THE EUROPEAN NOBILITY IN THE
EIGHTEENTH CENTURY

THE EUROPEAN NOBILITY
IN THE
EIGHTEENTH CENTURY

Studies of the Nobilities of
the major European states
in the pre-Reform Era

Edited by A. Goodwin, M.A.
Professor of Modern History in the
University of Manchester, and formerly
Fellow of Jesus College, Oxford

SECOND EDITION

ADAM & CHARLES BLACK
LONDON

FIRST PUBLISHED 1953
SECOND EDITION 1967
A. AND C. BLACK LIMITED
4, 5 AND 6 SOHO SQUARE LONDON W.1

SBN: 7136 0032 2

PRINTED IN THE UNITED STATES OF AMERICA

CONTENTS

PREFATORY NOTE

THIS revised edition of *The European Nobility in the Eighteenth Century* is, with the exception of one or two textual corrections and additional bibliographical references, essentially a reprint of a symposium of studies first published in 1953. Apart from Professor R. R. Palmer's *The Age of the Democratic Revolution. A Political History of Europe and America 1760–1800* Vol. I. *The Challenge* (Princeton, 1959)—which gives central importance to the role of the European aristocracies in the political evolution of the pre-revolutionary period—no major work of interpretative significance on the subject has since appeared. More recent research has modified views on the social and economic status of the several European nobilities in matters of detail, but it has, nevertheless, not been considered necessary to revise the original text for this new edition. It is hoped, however, that the supplementary bibliographical references to books and articles which have appeared since 1953 may enable students interested in the comparative social and constitutional history of Europe in the eighteenth century to become acquainted with the most recent work in this field.

For his willing co-operation in supplementing the bibliography on Poland by the late Professor Bruce Boswell I am indebted to Mr. L. R. Lewitter, Fellow of Christ's College and Lecturer in Slavonic Studies (Polish) in the University of Cambridge.

A. G.

PREFACE

Six of the essays included in this symposium were originally
delivered as a series of lectures in the University of Oxford in
the Hilary Term of 1952 by members of the Eighteenth Century
Group.[1] The other four have been contributed by scholars with
special knowledge of or interest in the history of the countries
concerned. No attempt has been made to follow a uniform
method of treatment, though the general aim of the symposium
is to facilitate a comparative view of the status and influence of
the major European aristocracies in the pre-Reform age.

Inevitably a slim volume, which attempts to deal with so
extended a field of inquiry, involving ten different countries at
different stages of development and each with its own peculiar
social structure and economic problems, must have serious
limitations. Generally speaking, within the space available to
them, contributors have not had the opportunity fully to develop ideas suggested by their own researches or by those of
others. Nor was it possible to include essays dealing with minor
states or countries. The Dutch burgher and Genevan aristocracies, the nobilities of Denmark, Portugal, the minor German
principalities and of the Italian states other than Lombardy, all
have claims to inclusion in any full study of the European
nobility of the eighteenth century. It might also have been
appropriate, in dealing with a period when cultural imitation
was a settled habit and fashionable vogue among the upper
strata of society, to have provided a general survey of the intellectual, cultural and social ties, which gave a semblance of unity
to the essential diversity of the European community. Except
where such themes have been touched on incidentally by individual contributors, they have had to be excluded. Similarly,

[1] Those on England, France, Lombardy, Prussia, Austria and Russia.

no attempt has been made to synthethize or to draw general conclusions.

Even with these limitations, however, such a collection of studies may perhaps serve a useful purpose in directing attention anew to the significant rôle played by the aristocracy in Europe in the period between the decline of seventeenth-century absolutism and the outbreak of the French revolution. It may also help to introduce English readers to issues and problems familiar enough to continental historians, but less widely appreciated in this country.

Each contributor has provided a select bibliography of his subject and these are, for convenience, collected together at the end of the book. In each of these some of the more important original sources and the more accessible secondary authorities are indicated, though here too the element of personal preference is as evident as in the points of view expressed in the essays themselves.

A. G.

I

ENGLAND

H. J. Habakkuk

IN continental countries, nobility was usually a status. The rights attaching to it varied from country to country, but it was reasonably clear in any particular country what the rights of a noble were and who was entitled to enjoy them. The outlines of the class were distinct and visible. In England there was no nobility in this strict sense. The nearest analogy was, perhaps, the class of families entitled to use armorial bearings, but while such bearings conferred social prestige, they did not convey privileges in respect of law, taxation, the ownership of land, or entry into the army and the church, nor, on the other hand, did they debar those who bore them from moving into trade and industry. These families were not marked off from their neighbours by a barrier of specific and identifiable privilege. And though, in some sense, they formed a social class, the outline of the class was, as de Tocqueville said, indistinct, and its limit unknown. Within this class there was, indeed, a group – the peers – distinguished by the right to sit in the House of Lords, and by certain privileges in law; and, in English usage, the word nobility became commonly restricted to the peers, as contrasted with the gentry. But the privileges of even this group were trivial: the right, for example, in criminal matters to be tried by their peers, or freedom from arrest upon mean process; they related only to the peer himself, and not to the members of his family; and they were much less important in distinguishing the peer from the commoner than the greater social prestige of the peer. Moreover, the group which enjoyed these privileges was much smaller than any continental nobility. In default of a precise counterpart, what class shall we examine? To accept what has become the normal usage and confine this essay to the aristocracy alone would be to sever a single, if not very homogeneous, social class, at a point which is not significant for the present purpose. I propose, therefore, to consider both the aristocracy and the gentry.

The basis of this class was the family estate, which provided the family not only with its revenue and its residence, but with its sense of identity from generation to generation. What was it that gave a landowner more general consequence than a moneyed man of equal wealth? Not only the visible fact of the rolling acres, the psychic ease which ownership of an estate conferred, the greater security of land, the control of tenantry at election times, but the fact that land could be made the vehicle of family purpose; its ownership could be determined for long periods ahead by the exercise of the general will of the family, in a way which was not true of other forms of property. What a merchant did with his money was primarily a matter for him alone. What a landowner did with his land was determined by a complex of decisions, in origin reaching far back into the family history, in effect stretching forward to his grandchildren yet unborn.

The descent of the typical English estate in the eighteenth century was governed by arrangements of immense complexity known as the strict settlement. These arrangements were most commonly made at the marriage of the heir, and they secured that the estate, or the greater part of it, descended intact to him, but descended on terms which greatly limited his power to sell and mortgage it. Once the deed of settlement was signed, the descent of the estate was settled for a generation ahead. Except by promoting a private Act of Parliament to break the settlement, there was no way by which the owner could obtain complete control of the estate until the eldest son of the marriage came of age. As a corollary, the settlement provided that the younger children of the marriage should receive annuities or capital sums charged upon the estate.

'A class which wishes to preserve its special powers and privileges', wrote J. L. and Barbara Hammond, 'has to discover some way of protecting its corporate interests from the misdemeanours and follies of individual members.' This function the strict settlement performed for the English landowners; in the long-term interests of the family it limited the immediate interests of its representative for the time being. Its rôle was, in some respects, analogous to that of the fidei commissum in the history of certain continental nobilities. It was, of course, less rigorous and binding than the fidei commissum, for it had to be repeated every generation: when the eldest son of the marriage came of age, it was open to him, in theory, to refuse to enter into another strict settlement, and though in fact he usually did so, the repetition depended on the recurrent exercise of the family will. Moreover, some of the smaller gentry did not adopt this form of settlement as a regular practice. Even families which normally settled their estates often excluded a substantial part from the settlement, and on occasion the whole estate might, by the accidents of family history, remain unsettled for considerable periods. But, loose and flexible as it was in comparison with the fidei commissum, the strict settlement did impede the sale or dispersion of estates, and certainly provided a more precise and uniform legal basis for the English landowning class that had existed in the century before 1640.

With the family estate went the family house, the physical expression of the standing of the family and the tangible repository of its traditions. When the founder of a new family replaced or rebuilt an adequate existing mansion, it was not solely because of changing taste or want of room, but because building a family home was an integral part of the founding of a family. There was no market in second-hand mansions in eighteenth-century England. The great house was also the centre of much of the life of the localities. The long corridors and enormous rooms were not mere ostentation; they were built to accommodate large households and the swarms of guests which descended on them at frequent intervals.' We used to sit down to dinner,' wrote Lord Hervey, in July 1731, of the company at Houghton, 'a little snug party of about thirty odd, up to the chin in beef, venison, geese, turkeys, etc.; and generally over the chin in claret, strong beer and punch. We had Lords Spiritual and Temporal, besides commoners, parsons and freeholders innumerable.' From some eighteenth century memoirs one might suppose that England was a federation of country houses.

Their families, houses and estates provided the daily routines of most English landowners. Many of them – but we do not know how many – went to London or to some provincial capital for the 'season'. The season indeed ranks with the strict settlement as a primary institution of the class, for it linked the country house, rural, patriarchal, and sometimes parochial, with the more elegant and diversified life of the urban drawing-room, refining the one and invigorating the other. But early in June, when the season was over, they went back to the country, to hunting and drinking, but not less to the absorbing minutiae of estate and household management. And it was in the country that even the greatest of them spent most of their time. If among the most rural of the country gentry there were few mere country bumpkins, even among the greater aristocracy there was none whose life was entirely divorced from the soil. Discussing with the steward the merits of tenants, rents, repairs and the management of timber was not a particularly strenuous occupation, but it gave landowners some real business to do. And country life gave them that stamina and bucolic vigour which they still exhibit in their portraits.

The largest item in the income of the aristocracy and gentry consisted of payments from tenant farmers, annual rack-rents, or sometimes, in the south-west and north, periodical lump sums called fines, which were calculated on the basis of the rack-rent value. Though several had home-farms, English land-owners did not, like landowners east of the Elbe, depend on the profits of direct farming; they were, and had long been rentiers. On the other hand they did not rely, as did some continental nobilities, on feudal dues; and the profits of manorial courts, quit-rents and copyhold rents provided a very small part of total income. Thus, in a sense, they had the best of both worlds. They were not farmers and therefore, like the French nobility and unlike the Junkers, they were a leisured class. None the less they were highly sensitive to changes in the fortunes of agriculture, they had an incentive to improve their estates – an incentive to which many responded – and their interests were directly and visibly linked with the prosperity of England's most important economic activity.

At what period these landowners began to draw a significant part of their income from urban and mining property is a question to which at present no satisfactory answer can be given. One of the few families which has been investigated in detail happens to have owned a great London estate. Miss Scott-Thomson has shown that the Bloomsbury estate of the Dukes of Bedford, which in 1732 yielded a gross return of £3700, by 1771 yielded about £8000, contributing, perhaps, between a third and a quarter of the family income. Other owners of London property, the Dukes of Portland, the Grosvenor family, the Pratts, the Comptons – possibly, too, owners of land in some provincial towns – must have profited in a similar way. In England common minerals were the property of the landowner, and several families owned mines. Some, like the Dudleys, worked them directly; others leased them to industrialists for long terms, and, as a class of men appeared who were capable of taking leases, this probably became the most usual method. It is easy enough to point to particular landed families who supplemented their incomes from the town and the mine, but difficult to judge how representative they were, since there were great variations from family to family and region to region. We know that in some regions, Durham, Stafford and Cornwall for example, the composition and fortunes of the class we are considering were greatly influenced by mineral wealth. But if I had to venture an opinion it would be that landowners who drew a significant part of their income from urban rents and minerals were still exceptional, and that most of even these landowners probably drew the greater part of their incomes from agriculture.

Probably a more important, and certainly a more widely diffused supplement to landed incomes was income from offices. It was one of the main charges of the writers who in the early nineteenth century attacked the whole aristocratic system that the governing class had farmed itself out on the public revenue. No one has yet examined systematically the contribution which political and administrative office made to landed incomes, and indeed no precise estimate would be possible since a large part of the emoluments often consisted of fees which fluctuated with the business of the office. But clearly, the emoluments of the major government posts were considerable, particularly in time of war. It was estimated that from 1747 to 1753 the clear profits of the office of Secretary of State amounted to an average of £5780 a year. The value of the office in 1762 was put at £8000 or £9000 a year. Nor need gains cease with office. In 1756 the Earl of Waldgrave, refusing a pension of £2000 a year for life, asked for the reversion of one of the very lucrative Tellerships of the Exchequer. When Lord Holdernesse was turned out of the office of Secretary of State in 1761, he was given the reversion of the Wardenship of the Cinque Ports, and a pension of £4000 a year in the meantime. Several peers, moreover, held court offices, the salaries of which were often supplemented by pensions and annuities; and salaries, while less permanent than incomes from land, were subject to far fewer deductions. What the net gains really were we do not know. Much of the money from offices, no doubt, went to maintain the style of life appropriate to the office; but some sometimes went to promote the long-term interests of the family. A friend observed of George Grenville that it was his unvaried practice 'in all situations . . . to live on his own private fortune, and save the emoluments of whatever office he possessed'.

What a Teller's place was for a family of importance, a minor post in the Customs, the Excise, or the Tax Office might be for a lesser one. But in calculating what official incomes meant to landed families, whether great or small, it is not only the direct addition to the income of the head of the family which is relevant. Offices were, par excellence, a way of providing for the younger sons. This indeed was the crux of the attack. 'The aristocracy, usurping the power of the state, have the means under various pretexts of extorting for the junior branches of their families a forced subsistence.' And when one looks at the Walpole family, one is not disposed to write off such language as baseless rhetoric. At Walpole's death, his eldest son held among other offices the Auditorship of the Exchequer, valued at £7000 a year. His second son, Edward, was Clerk of the Pells, and derived from this office £3000 a year. Horace Walpole held offices which, Mr Ketton-Cremer has estimated, were worth, after his father died, approximately £3400 a year. Contemporary correspondence, which teems with references to places and offices, gives the impression that, if the scale of this provision was unusually lavish, there was nothing unusual about the method.

Were English landed families, as a whole, affluent? Did they, on balance, save? Some families were notoriously wealthy; Lord Temple, as he himself modestly observed, 'had a great deal of money to spare'; William Pulteney left over a million; the second Lord Foley was reputed to have left in 1766 real estate worth £21,000 a year, mines worth £7000 a year and £500,000 in the funds. But others of the same class were heavily in debt; in 1741, for example, the second Lord Weymouth, whose income, excluding jointures and annuities, was £12,000 per annum, owed £100,000 on mortgages and bonds, and had book debts amounting to about £30,000. There was immense variation, not only from family to family but within a single family. In the course of a century, the same family might be affluent at one time and heavily indebted at another. A single profligate – and sooner or later one cropped up in most families – might quickly ravage the family fortunes. Even families who escaped this affliction were at the mercy of birth and death rates; in some generations many children survived, in others few; some wives died before their husbands, others long survived them. A bevy of healthy but ineligible daughters, a hardy and well-jointured dowager might do more damage to a family than the gaming table, as witness the wife of the third Duke of Leeds who survived her husband sixty-three years and drew £190,000 in jointure from the estate. Conversely, few children and the absence of a dowager might allow a family to accumulate considerable wealth. Apart, too, from these demographic vagaries, there was a natural history of families. The first generation might inherit money as well as land from the founding father, and sometimes, too, economical habits. In succeeding generations the family was apt to acquire the characteristic habits of the class into which it had risen; it exhausted the reserves, accumulated debt, and became increasingly vulnerable to changes in economic climate. This was a tendency only, which might be checked or reversed by a variety of circumstances; vast estates and wide connections gave the great families a certain immunity, but the tendency is clearly visible in the rise and decline of families among the smaller gentry.

We must therefore expect the facts, when they are established, to reveal very great variety of family circumstances. But the best opinion, that of Malthus for example, assumed that landowners were pre-eminently consumers. And this still remains the most reasonable generalization. Certainly, among the typical landed families of midland England, the greater part of the income was absorbed in current expenditure, taxation, interest payments, and in annuities to members of the family, annuities which in their turn were spent primarily on current consumption. Only when the family built or enlarged the great house did capital expenditure absorb a large part of their resources. Expenditure on improvements, important as this expenditure may have been for agriculture, appears in most cases to have been relatively small; and except in the case of recently established families who had not laid out all their original fortune in land, any holdings in government funds were usually modest. Landowners were indeed characteristically the borrowing class, and the greater part of their mortgages in this century were not for productive enterprise, but to provide portions for their daughters or to fund short-term debts incurred in periods of living beyond their income. Though the more affluent members of the class are to be found among the lenders, most of the loans were provided by lawyers, merchants and by what was known in contemporary parlance as the monied interest.

We must not adopt a middle-class attitude to the debts of landowning families. Mortgages which at first sight seem overwhelming were in fact light in relation to the capital value of the estate, sometimes very much less burdensome than the mortgages which even provident dons incur on their homes. Still less must we assume that shortage of ready money is a sign of imminent disaster. Individual members of a family might temporarily be very short of cash, though their long-term position, still more than of their family as a whole, was entirely secure. No doubt some families were forced to sell a substantial part of their property; and in many cases the burden of debt made rapid adjustment to changes of circumstances extremely difficult. At one time or other in the century the finances of a number of very substantial families fell into confusion. But there was always a possibility that the next generation would be small, and in the last resort these families could, like Sir Walter Elliot of Kellynch Hall, lease the house to Admiral Croft and go off and retrench in Bath.

Did the general economic position of this class improve during the eighteenth century? There is no reasonable doubt that circumstances were more favourable to landed incomes in the century after 1715 than they had been between 1640 and 1715. Under the stimulus of agrarian improvements, particularly those associated with enclosures, of increasing population, of growing trade and industry, there was a substantial rise of rents; there were variations from region to region and even from estate to estate, but the rise was visible in most parts of the country about the middle of the century, became rapid about the 1770's and spectacular during the wars against Revolutionary and Napoleonic France. Moreover, down at least to Pitt's Income Tax, taxation was less severe than in the seventy years before 1715. When Malthus argued that 'in the progress of a country towards a higher state of improvement, the positive wealth of the landlord ought . . . gradually to increase,' he was as much generalizing from history as deducing from theory.

What we do not know is how far this rise in income was offset by an increase in expenditure. About the 1770's there is a perceptible change in the social climate, of which the most obvious mark is the increase in speculation and gambling. The position of the eldest son – relatively poor while his father lived but certain at his father's death to inherit the estate – was always the point of weakness in the system of family management that rested on the strict settlement; in limiting the power of the owner to damage the estate, the settlement deprived him of the power to discipline his children. But in the 60's and 70's the temptation to 'show the spirit of an heir' seems to have grown stronger, and a good deal of wealth wandered as a result. There was a great increase in the sale of annuities for the life of the seller, a method by which a person of little immediate substance could borrow considerable amounts on terms which often proved disastrous. The two elder sons of the third Lord Foley by this means borrowed £100,000 to pay their gambling debts, and permanently impaired the fortunes of their family. Moreover, even when we have no evidence of such spectacular gambling debts, the increase in expenditure appears to have been rapid. The household and miscellaneous expenditure of the Duke of Portland rose from £4000 in 1784 to £12,000 in 1797, £21,000 in 1801, and, after dropping to £12,000 in 1803, rose to £38,000 in 1805. Apart from any change in the tastes of landowners, mortgages incurred to provide portions for daughters tended to accumulate. They were charges on the estate, not on the owner for the time being, who therefore lacked an incentive to pay them off out of his current income. Every generation of daughters brought additional mortgages, and, in the course of a century or so, many were raised and few repaid. Within the very organization of a landed family, therefore, there was a mechanism which persistently worked for an increase in the family debt. Finally, on the income side, it might be long before landowners obtained the full advantage of urban and mineral properties which were let on long leases. The nucleus of what became the Dowlais iron-works was let by the Windsor family for 99 years at a rent of £31 a year; when the lease expired in 1848, it was renewed at a rent in the neighbourhood of £25,000 a year. For almost a century the enormous increase in the value of the property had accrued not to the landowner but to the industrialists who leased it.

What was the place of this class in the political arrangements of the period? In many continental states, a characteristic problem of the eighteenth century was how to reconcile the nobility to the rise of bureaucratic absolutism, which was sometimes also the problem of how to reconcile the localities to the growth of central power. Such problems did not exist in England. Not only because the landowners were not an order of society, with privileges which could be infringed and had to be defended, but because the English landowners were the governing class of the country. Ministers were drawn usually from the great families, and though the property qualifications imposed by the Act of 1711 were easily evaded, the normal social and political processes ensured that most M.P.'s came from landed families. Local government likewise was in the hands, not of a bureaucracy, but of Justices of the Peace, who were generally landowners. The land tax was administered by the same class, and even in those departments which were run by professionals, the more important and dignified posts were often filled from landowning families.

There was, indeed, a traditional opposition between the country gentlemen who prevailed in local administration and the Court and central government, and this opposition was not without political and social importance, but, because land-owning families dominated in both spheres, it did not become open conflict over specific rights. The period between the end of active conciliar intervention in the seventeenth century and the revival of central direction in the early nineteenth was pre-eminently a period of local autonomy. The initiative in dealing with new social and economic problems was taken, if taken at all, in the locality, partly by the promotion of private acts to establish turnpikes, build canals, etc., but probably as much in the course of administering the existing law. The great ex-tension of outdoor poor relief at the end of the century, for example, resulted from administrative decisions taken by Justices in Quarter Sessions, who were neither stimulated nor controlled by the central government. The machinery of local government in the eighteenth century had notorious short-comings, and in the latter part of the period there was a rapid increase in problems which local initiative either could or would not deal with. Nevertheless, to the end of the century the Justices remained the most active organs of adaptation in English society.

In the army, the navy and the church, success depended on anything which would give a man influence – wealth, family, friendships and abilities of every kind; and no single one of these was overriding. In such a society it was possible for men of low social origins to rise to prominence; and in so far as landed families did in fact predominate in these occupations, it was because of wealth, connection or aptitude, and not because of prescriptive right or birth. The predominance was most marked in the army. The higher officers were usually the younger sons of landowning families, or the sons of younger sons. Among the English generals in the war against the American colonies, for example, Howe and Gage were the second sons of Irish Viscounts, Clinton was the only son of the second son of an Earl of Lincoln, and Burgoyne the only son of a younger son of a wealthy baronet family. It was difficult for men of moderate means to attain high rank since commissions had to be purchased, but the higher ranks were open to anyone with the necessary money; and if no sons of merchants are to be found among our generals, it is primarily due, not to social exclusiveness, but to the feeling, by no means confined to the landed families or to the eighteenth century, that by upbringing and aptitude the sons of landed families were likely to make the best military leaders. The navy was more democratic, and political influence and considerations of birth, though certainly not negligible, were curbed by the more exacting demands of naval service; it was more difficult to handle a ship than a regiment. The second son into the army, the third into the church: this was a traditional fate of younger sons. Since landowners owned the right of presentation to many livings, their connection with the church was more intimate than with any other profession, and the rise of the 'squarson' suggests that in the eighteenth century it was becoming closer. Many of the bishops, too, North and Barrington, for example, came from landed families, though they sat side by side on the Bishop's Bench with several of humble birth, since a great man's chaplain might by influence rise as high as a great man's brother.

The grades of title within the landowning class from Duke down to plain gentry were primarily social gradings. They probably corresponded in a very rough and ready way with gradations of landed wealth, and there was a general notion of the estate appropriate to maintain a given rank. But there was no sharp break in wealth between the higher ranges of one rank and the lower ranges of the next, and there was indeed a fringe of impoverished peers and baronets who had inherited the title but not the estate. Even the line of division between peers and commoners – a line to which, judging by the efforts made to cross it, contemporaries attached importance – was not a decisive one. The attempt to make the peerage an exclusive caste, the Peerage Bill of 1719, failed and was in any event a political manœuvre rather than a product of class feeling.

Nevertheless, within the peerage itself, there was a group of great families clearly distinguished in point of wealth and influence from other landowning families, 'the great oaks that shade a country', as Burke described them. Their origins were miscellaneous, but a high proportion were founded with fortunes made in government service, and many were descended from Tudor 'new men', who had acquired monastic property. If the dissolution of the monasteries contributed to the rise of the gentry, it was no less a formative episode in the history of the modern English aristocracy, as one can see from a distribution map of the great eighteenth-century estates. Like the House of Austria, these families extended their estates by fortunate marriages, and in the eighteenth century they owned large properties, often scattered over several counties. A number of them, the Devonshire family, for example, the Rockinghams, Egremonts, Shelburnes and Hertfords, had also considerable estates in Ireland. Many of these families were linked together by an intricate network of intermarriage, so that sometimes they bore the appearance more of tribes than of families.

Sir Lewis Namier has shown that the electoral influence of the great families has been exaggerated; at the accession of George III, even such a grandee as the Duke of Bedford had only four boroughs at his disposal, the Duke of Devonshire only three and several of the Dukes none at all. In respect of borough patronage there was no line of division between the great families and the rest of the peers, nor between peers and commoners. Nor in the counties did the territorial magnates exert unchallenged dominance, but divided their power with the gentlemen of the county. Moreover, their influence reflected the geographical distribution of the great houses; their characteristic spheres of influence were the north, the northern midlands and some of the eastern counties. The south-west and west were areas of smaller properties, and there the social and political influence of the gentry was relatively greater. But electoral influence does not fully measure the political significance of the great families. A large part of English history has consisted of the relations of Crown, magnates and gentry. The relations between Crown and magnates have usually involved elements of partnership as well as conflict. And, though the nature of the binding ties has varied, the magnates have usually been the centres of groups and connections bound together by ties of blood, friendship and obligation. What distinguishes the eighteenth century is that, in their partnership with the Crown, the magnates were more powerful than in previous periods, and that the aristocratic connection was a more integral part of political arrangements. It would be absurd to suppose that these families had a monopoly of political power, if only because the greatest statesmen of the century were not, in fact, drawn from their ranks. Yet, by reason of their great stake in the country, and their long and close association with government, they bore a heavier responsibility for the fame and fortune of the country than did the rest of the political nation. And, as Miss Sutherland has suggested, it was because English politics were dominated by such families, 'whose main source of riches remained outside the sphere of politics' and who 'in the last resort felt some responsibility for, and interest in the maintenance of the king's government', that influence, interest and connection did not prove incompatible with ordered government.

According to the traditional view, this aristocracy was more intimately linked with other social classes, the bourgeoisie in particular, than were the aristocracies of the Continent; it recruited itself from talent displayed and wealth acquired in the professions, and sent back into the professions the families of its younger sons. Of the broad truth of this view there can be no doubt. In England political power and social standing depended to a greater extent than elsewhere on the ownership of landed property as opposed to lineage or royal favour. Since there were no legal restrictions on the right to acquire land, any man, however humble his origin, who had enough money

might purchase an estate, and thereby acquire social consequence. And not only was it easy for wealthy bourgeois to
acquire an estate; in relation to the landowners there were
more of them than on the Continent. For all these reasons the
English landed class was constantly recruiting new members.
Because Englishmen who had made fortunes in law, government or trade transformed themselves into country gentlemen,
England had no urban aristocracy on the Dutch model. There
were wealthy merchants but few mercantile dynasties, and the
great London houses were the town houses of the landed
nobility. It would indeed be difficult to exaggerate the wider
social repercussions of this flow into landownership.

We know very little, however, about the speed of this flow
during the eighteenth century, and it is often exaggerated. For
lawyers, merchants and other 'new men' could buy estates
only if established landowners were prepared to sell; established
landowners for the most part only sold when they had to; and,
it may well be argued, during the eighteenth century the
occasions when landowners had to sell were less frequent than
in the seventeenth century. It does indeed appear that in the
two or three decades after 1715 a large number of estates were
sold – an aftermath, perhaps of high war taxes, and sometimes
even of Commonwealth impositions – but in the second half
of the century, when rents were buoyant, the land tax light
and political impositions absent, there were times when would-
be purchasers found it very difficult to find the estates they
wanted, and it is possible, though it cannot be put any higher,
that there was a slackening in the rate at which new families
were recruited. Whatever the merits of this suggestion, it is
clear that few individuals, except perhaps Paymaster-Generals
in time of war, were able to make in a single lifetime enough
money to buy an estate as large as those of the greater aristocracy, many of which represented the accumulation of several
generations.

Furthermore, while it was easier in England for a man of
humble birth and great fortune to acquire considerable landed

property and a title, there might be a long time-lag between the acquisition of the property and its recognition by a title. The English peerage in the eighteenth century was not as accessible to mere wealth, even to landed wealth, as one is apt to suppose. It must not be assumed that it was easily accessible merely because it was not a status; the privileges of a nobility, their scope, and the precision with which they are defined, are one question, the ease with which nobility is acquired is quite another. The creation of peers rested with the monarch, who might have prejudices or convictions in the matter. Until the burst of new creations of 1784, the peerage remained a small body, and the new creations were little more than enough to replace peerages which had become extinct. There were 161 temporal peers in 1704 and 182 in 1780, excluding the representative Scottish peers. The number of new creations was indeed larger than this might suggest, for the mortality among noble families in the eighteenth century was high; of the forty-five peerages created by Anne, thirteen had become extinct before 1784. Still, by most standards the number of new creations was small. Anne created thirty new peerages (apart, that is, from promotions within the peerage), George I twenty-eight and George II thirty-nine; in the first twenty-three years of his reign, George III created forty-seven. George III was jealous of the honour of the peerage. As he wrote to Bute after refusing Egremont's request for a Marquisate, 'I looked on our Peerage as the most honourable of any country, and I never would hurt it by putting the juniors of them over the seniors'.

But more significant for our present purpose than the number is the character of the new peers. The largest single group consisted of men ennobled for service to the state; statesmen like Walpole and Pitt, politicians of second rank like Speaker Onslow and George Lyttleton, lawyers like Cowper, Harcourt and Macclesfield, soldiers like Cadogan and Cobham, sailors like Hawke and Rodney; of these only the lawyers can properly be said to represent new men. Another group, not entirely exclusive of the first, consisted of the sons of peers, men who had acquired a claim to titles by marrying into the families which had borne them in some previous period, Irish peers and baronets of old landed families. All these were men to whom a peerage was only one step in promotion. The peer of obscure social origin was rare, and there were none who had been actively engaged in trade, nor, until Smith was made Lord Carrington, was there any financier. The great merchants and financiers were rewarded less lavishly, by baronetcies or by Irish peerages. In 1784 an exceptionally large number of new peerages was created, which did radically change the size of the English peerage. But even then it was not, *pace* Disraeli, from 'the alleys of Lombard Street and the counting-houses of Cornhill' that the new peers were drawn, but predominantly from among the older and more substantial families of squires.

It is true that even the oldest of the families raised to the peerage in the eighteenth century were recent by continental standards, and indeed that the greater aristocracy themselves were of no great antiquity. Because of the high mortality in the Wars of the Roses and the proscriptions of the Tudors, there were few survivors of the mediaeval nobility. England was not, of course, alone in this respect. If many of the great English families were established in the sixteenth century, many of the Austrian nobility were not established till the seventeenth. But granted the relatively recent origin of many of our great families, what does it tell us about them? According to one historian, that 'the aristocracy of eighteenth century England was really little more than a wealthier middle class'. We must not, having renounced the legend that they were an oligarchy, substitute the much less plausible legend that families like the Fitzwilliams, the Russells, the Leveson-Gowers, the Seymours were a middle class. In their wealth, style of living, social standing and habits of mind, the great English families were an aristocracy, a separate species, but of the same genus as the greater families of the Continent. The English memory for social origins was, indeed, shorter than was general on the Continent; since few families were very old, newcomers were less conspicuously new. But social origins were not forgotten. On this point the catholicity of English social life is apt to mislead. London society was open to the amusing, the talented and the able; the visible signs of rank and birth which, in German states for example, inhibited social intercourse were absent here. But the marriages of a class are a better index of its social feelings than the composition of its dinner parties. And few children of the great families married into families far removed from them in rank and general standing. There were, of course, marriages between aristocrats and bourgeois heiresses. No one has yet calculated their frequency, but it is evident from the terms of the settlements on such marriages that considerable material gains were necessary to induce the great families to contract them, and, when the relevant statistics are available, we may perhaps find that actresses were not much less common than bourgeois heiresses. The contemporary attention which mésalliances commanded is proof of their rarity rather than of their frequency; they were sufficiently frequent to provide a plausible theme for novel and play, but sufficiently rare to prove an interesting one. When the daughter of the Duke of Richmond, flouting her parents' wishes, married Henry Fox . . . 'I thought,' said Carteret, 'our fleet or our army were beat, or Mons betrayed into the hands of the French.'

The closest links with other social classes were provided not by incoming peers, but by outgoing younger sons. Reservations must be made even here. Voltaire observed that in England a peer's brother did not think trade beneath him, but added, 'this custom . . . begins to be laid aside'. It was, in fact, extremely rare for a younger son of a peer to go into trade. Most of them went into the army or the church, or were provided with pensions and places. It was only among the gentry with large families that trade was at all a common occupation for a younger son. And though the fact that younger sons contributed their energies and abilities to the professions is immensely important, it may well be argued that their departure from the family hearth was as much a condition of the wealth and superiority of the main line of the family as it was a link with other social groups. The real distinguishing feature of English society was that even had these cadet branches of great families remained aristocratic they would not have been marked off from their fellows by a barrier of privilege. If in England the relations of the aristocracy and the middle classes did not constitute a problem, it was not because the aristocracy were bourgeois – far from it – but because the exclusive rights of the nobility which created the problem on the Continent did not exist in this country. There were divergencies of economic interests, and wide differences in way of life and mental habit, but, except for the game laws, economic and social differences were not accentuated by differences of legal right.

I do not intend to discuss the morals and habits of the aristocracy. These are embalmed in Horace Walpole's letters. Wealth and leisure are likely to produce great diversity of character and taste, and among the aristocracy of this period were architects, philosophers, scientists, agricultural improvers and every type of character from the rake to the puritan. But unless the members of such a class are restrained by religious feeling or strong moral conventions, their lowest common denominator is apt to be dissoluteness of manners. Gout was the occupational disease of the English aristocracy, and mistresses a frequent by-product of their arranged marriages. Dissoluteness did not, however, mean breakdown of character as often as it does among classes subject to more rigorous moral codes, and it by no means implied absence of refined taste and feeling. The eighteenth-century aristocracy were probably more widely cultivated than their seventeenth-century predecessors. The Grand Tour, by the mid-century an established rite, whatever it did for their morals, polished their manners, enlarged their interests and educated their taste. Vanbrough and the brothers Adam built their houses; Chippendale and Sheraton designed their furniture; Reynolds and Gainsborough painted their portraits. As Voltaire remarked, and as their libraries suggest, they esteemed learning and literature, in a gentlemanly sort of way; and if in the course of the century the growth of a middle-class reading public diminished the importance of the individual aristocrat as a patron of letters, they continued to set the public taste in the visual arts.

But the most important single fact about the English nobility is that they were, in the locality and at the centre, the politically effective class, and therefore felt a responsibility for the way things went. They were prepared to tax themselves, and in the two great wars against France to tax themselves heavily. The Hammonds conclude a sustained indictment of the activities of the enclosing English landlords with this reluctant tribute: 'The other European aristocracies crumbled at once before Napoleon: the English aristocracy amid all its blunders and errors kept its character for endurance and fortitude.'

2

FRANCE

J. McManners

FRANCE on the eve of the Revolution was a country of bewildering social divisions. In March 1789 Mallet du Pan wrote
to Dumont, 'The divided orders subdivide still further, the
trunks bear branches that diverge to every point of the compass.
There is the upper, middle and lower clergy, the enfeoffed
nobility and the non-feudal nobility, the privileged, the parlements, then the upper third estate and the lower, then the
provinces under one form of government and the provinces
under another.' It was no longer possible to describe France in
the simple terms of the three orders of clergy, nobility and
third estate, for this horizontal stratification of society was now
in dissolution, and confusing cross-divisions and vertical rifts
were appearing in the structure. Thus, the quarter of a million
individuals (taking an average figure between widely differing
estimates) who together formed the nobility of France cannot
be considered as a simple collective unity, for they formed an
order which contained within itself a vastly graded hierarchy,
and which was, in any case, disintegrating under the tension of
new social forces; there was one trunk, but, as Mallet du Pan
observed, the divergent branches spring out in every direction.

One might begin the analysis of the structure of the nobility
by referring to the three categories used by the jurists of the
eighteenth century, based on methods of acquiring noble status.
Firstly, there was *noblesse de race*, hereditary nobility transmitted
from the father, and in certain provinces from the mother,
though this uterine nobility was of doubtful status. Secondly,

there was *noblesse de lettres* requiring registration in the *Chambre des Comptes*, where the fee was paid, and thirdly, there was *noblesse de dignité*, conveyed by the holding of office. This *noblesse de dignité* may be divided into the *noblesse de robe*, at the highest point of which stand the officers of the sovereign courts, who had obtained personal nobility in the sixteenth century and hereditary nobility in the seventeenth, and also the *noblesse de cloche*, derived from the exercise of municipal offices in certain towns. The lawyers, however, held that these categories were of purely historical importance, and that among the nobility there should be no differences but those of lineage. As the standard law dictionary of 1781 has it, 'All nobles hold their prerogative from the king, there is no difference between them save in the antiquity of their origin' – which is, of course, the attitude one would expect from the *noblesse de robe*, who were not disposed to admit any inherent inferiority in their own status. In practice, the official method of testing nobility corresponded to this contention of the lawyers. The test of nobility generally, 'old' nobility, such as was required for entrance to the *École Militaire*, was the test of four generations. Excluded by this test are the newly ennobled, and beyond this outer circle lies the penumbra of those Le Bret calls 'demi-noblesse', who hold offices conferring certain noble privileges but not the actual status, such as army officers exempt from the *taille* after twenty years' service, or *avocats* enjoying exemption from the militia. The routine test of four generations was not, however, adequate for formal presentation at court; for this, one must belong to the old feudal nobility, and the caste requirements were finally formulated in the regulation of 1760, which made the year 1400 the dead-line. According to Chérin, the official genealogist, there were less than a thousand families in this category. The names are not all great names of the court like the La Luzernes and the de Ségurs; the chevalier de Chateaubriand passed the test, and had the privilege of spoiling Louis XVI's aim when hunting and hearing five words from the royal lips. Those of the higher social set who were excluded felt their position bitterly – Mme Grimod de la Reynière could not bear to hear the very name of Versailles mentioned – and the barrier was most irksome to the great families of the magistracy, who, says Sénac de Meilhan, found themselves treated like parish councillors by the feudal nobility on the strength of a distinction which only arose in the reign of Louis XIV.

Here at Versailles we may study the hierarchy at the very summit of the social pyramid. First come the *enfants de France*, that is, the children and grandchildren (and sometimes the nephews) of the reigning monarch, followed by the princes of the blood, and after these, among the rest of the nobility, precedence was derived from dignities conferred by the crown. First in rank were the *pairs*, the peers of France, comprising, in addition to the princes of the blood, seven bishops and nearly fifty *ducs*, who played a traditional rôle at the coronation, enjoyed ceremonial distinctions in royal houses, and had the right to sit in the Parlement of Paris, provided they had been received there, a privilege which some were too indifferent to exercise. These were spendthrift days, and special regulations allowed the heir to a peerage to purchase the lands of the duchy on favourable terms, to ensure that they were not mortgaged away into the general mass of noble property. Next in the hierarchy came the few *ducs* who were not peers, and those who held the dignity for life only by royal brevet, then marquises and counts. Alongside this scale of ranks, the marshals of France enjoyed the unique distinction of judging disputes of honour among the nobility. Such was the order of precedence, and wherever there was a gap in the regulations, battle was waged at Versailles. The refusal of the great to subordinate themselves to a cardinal disrupted the councils of the Regency, the princes of the blood suppressed the archbishop of Cambrai's title of 'serene highness', the *ducs* fought continuously against the pretensions of the princes of Lorraine and of the legitimized natural descendants of Louis XIV. To take the fortunes of the *ducs* in a single year: in March 1744 the peers memorialized the king against the machinations of the *légitimés*; in the following month the *ducs* upbraided the mother of the boy duc d'Antin for allowing her son to wander into the Maunday Thursday feet-washing ceremony, which was under boycott on a point of precedence; in June they lamented the breakdown of the regulations which had given duchesses the monopoly of parasols at the Corpus Christi procession, and finally, at the funeral of the maréchal de Chaulnes in November, they consolidated an old victory over the marshals of France.

So the empty struggle (empty except in so far as a connection with the pensions list is involved) for precedence round the throne continued, yet, more and more as the century progressed, the great nobles were turning, for their pleasures and socially significant activities, not to Versailles, but to Paris. In France, state and society, the crown and the economically dominant classes, Versailles and Paris were falling apart, and the fantastic caste system which is embalmed for ever in the seventeen volumes of protocol and ceremony of the good duc de Luynes was every day becoming more obsolete. Men still insisted, insisted more than ever, on defining and re-defining the qualifications for each rung of the ladder, yet all the while trade, industry, finance and culture were building a new and more permanent stairway. A social revolution was in progress, and the centre of this revolution was in Paris.

In the high society of the capital the futility of caste barriers founded on birth alone was becoming obvious, and in a fashion the egalitarian and reformist tendencies among the nobility, which we must consider later, were a reflex action produced by this realization, an indirect admission of the fact. As a reaction against the parvenu who was flaunting his title of baron or marquis, the genuine old nobility were signing their names only, while the masked ball is the typical Parisian divertissement of a class with an uneasy conscience, clinging to privileges it has ceased to believe in. The *collèges* of the old régime did not treat noble and bourgeois equally, but they gave both the same education. This lesson was continued in the *salon*, where wit held a priority which mere birth could not obtain. Duclos, enforcing academic equality against the maréchal de Belle-Isle and the comte de Clermont, was defending his ideal that 'letters should form a republic, of which liberty is the soul', and Voltaire, after receiving the bastinado which was the only revenge ancestry could take on ability, had achieved an empire which put him beyond the reach of a chevalier de Rohan-Chabot. Above all else, in society at large, an even greater power than wit dominated, and more and more the true hierarchy of society was seen to be based upon its possession. That power was money. Money is the key to the understanding of French society in the eighteenth century. With the power of money behind it, the plutocracy was infiltrating into the aristocracy. (One uses the word 'plutocracy' deliberately, to avoid discussion of the subdivisions of the 'bourgeoisie', a word which in itself lumps fortunes together at the very point where their dividing line is sociologically significant, and confounds those who envy and infiltrate with those who envy hopelessly.) This movement of the plutocracy into the aristocracy is not surprising. For a long time in France most things depending on the government had been up for sale. The magistrature had bought its offices, even if sufficiently long ago to be respectable now; the brevets of captain and above in the army were for sale, and were bought, often enough, by the sons of the newly ennobled; and musty cobwebs to drape bottles of raw and recent vintage could be conveniently spun in the elaborate forgers' workshops in Avignon and the Comté Venaisson.

Marriage, the principal unifying factor in society, was based avowedly on money. Continual intermarriage had made the wealthy magistrature practically at one with the higher nobility and drew both towards the financiers, so that, as Chamfort observed, 'almost all the women of any position, either in Versailles or Paris, are only upper middle class'. Financiers, whether they became technically ennobled by purchasing an office of *secrétaire du roi* or not, lived nobly. The typical Farmer-

General is not a 'bourgeois gentilhomme', but a dignified and responsible official, with every claim to move in the highest circles. The son of a financier, born in Paris in 1768, writes, 'My family belonged to high finance, a class which had become a sort of dignity in the state since Louis XIV's quest for glory had ruined the nobility, and the folly of the Regent had handed the public fortune over to the money dealers, and since big fortunes and high birth had intermarried. The philosophers completed the levelling process, and there were few dignities in the state which ranked higher than the brevet of a Farmer General or a chair at the Academy.' Intermarriage is not the only sign of the interpenetration of classes. The court nobility were engaging in big financial and industrial enterprises on their own account. Employment as a magistrate was not averse to them: witness the career of Hérault de Séchelles, of noble lineage going back to 1390, cousin of the comtesse de Polignac (the friend of Marie-Antoinette) and of the comtesse de Polastron (mistress of the comte d'Artois), who, with favourable winds from Versailles, was *avocat général* in the Parlement of Paris at the age of twenty-six. On the other hand the nobility of the magistrature aped the nobility of the court and plunged into fashionable dissipations; we hear of the président Lepelletier's clandestine suppers, and of the nocturnal promenades in the Palais Royal of the *premier avocat général* Séguier. 'A young magistrate', Mercier observes, 'fears nothing so much as to be known for what he really is. He talks horses, theatre, women, racing, battles. He blushes to admit a knowledge of his profession.' The pleasures of high society were common to the wealthy. 'Gaming and wit', said Talleyrand, 'had levelled everything.' There was, too, a common intellectual atmosphere. From this social situation at the end of the old régime sprang a liberal movement in which each class had its share. In Duport's *Société des Trente* great nobles, magistrates of the Parlement and bankers rubbed shoulders, and Ferrières even ascribes the liberalism of the deputies of the nobles of Paris to the Estates General to their 'liaisons with the capitalists', which gave them 'interests differing from those of the nobility generally'.

Thus, while the geographical survey of Paris shows the great nobility resident in the *faubourg St.-Germain*, the aristocracy of the law in the austere *quartier du Marais*, and the high financiers around the Palais-Royal and the Tuilleries, the social map of the capital reveals a single society, united by riches. The overall picture is not that of a caste of nobility graded by antiquity of lineage, but of an upper class unified by money, divided into caste strata whose particular blazons are sought after as admission tickets to lucrative employments or favours, or for their snob value, or simply as collector's pieces.

Unlike the magistrates and the financiers, the great nobles who were rich enough to spend their time in the high society of Versailles and the capital – those two contrasting worlds – were a class which had lost its true rôle in the state. It is often said that the rise of royal absolutism under Louis XIV had driven them into intrigue and dissipation as a substitute for true political activity. In a famous passage, Taine describes the court as a flask of gold and crystal – to fill it with perfume, a great nobility must be made barren of fruit, and bear only flowers. And yet, when the nobility did have their chance to share in the government of the state under the Regency, they failed miserably. Their financial manœuvres, their foolish disputes over precedence and their general selfish incoherence reveal what their idea of government really was; it was of the last Regency and of the Fronde that they were thinking, of the politics described in the recently published memoirs of Mme de Moteville and the cardinal de Retz. There were opportunities for public service in the episcopate and in embassies, and for ministers, the crown took ability where it found it, given reasonable loyalty, whether that be in political cardinals at the beginning of the century or in the nobility of the magistrature at the end. Of Louis XVI's thirty-six ministers, all except one are noble, but only three are of the old feudal families, while twenty-six are of families of the ennobled magistracy. The collapse of moral standards among the *noblesse*

dorée, the gilded nobility of the Court, may be due originally
to their unemployment, but it is more certain that their continued unemployment was due to the collapse of their moral
standards. Their situation in the army may be used as the acid
test. War was their ancestors' profession, and the higher commands were still theirs for the asking, witness the five *ducs* and
one prince among the eleven marshals of 1789. They rejoiced
in the cachet of military position. They were brave enough in
action, but they did not learn the trade of war. The famous
Maison du Roi became a unit of the antechamber, and the defeats
of the century, Rossbach in particular, redound to the discredit
of the dilettante soldier. 'Have you seen any fugitives?' asked
prince Louis de Bourbon Condé, ecclesiastical pluralist and
general, fleeing from the stricken field. 'Non, Monseigneur,
vous êtes le premier.' The famous 'douceur de vivre' of the
old régime was concocted from a very simple formula, privilege without responsibility.

The pensions list, even more than the army list, bears testimony to the parasitism of the great. It is a sorry record of
absurd offices, pointless pensions and unwarranted compen-
sations – the Grand Admiral's anchorage dues, the fees to the
Mistress of the Queen's Household, the 'widows and orphans'
fund' that kept the wolf from the door of the duc d'Ayen and
the princesse de Carignan. Contemptuous of the sordid details,
the court nobility were nevertheless greatly concerned with
money-making. D'Argenson's candid memoirs give us the
inside story of a man with a position to keep up. He complains
that his father didn't even leave him a silver fork and had
pushed him into a marriage which proved financially dis-
appointing, and yet, he boasts, I paid off my youthful debts,
furnished a house at Paris and the *château*, educated two children, gave back my wife's dowry, bought back my father's
library, collected medals and engravings, all at the expense of
only 200,000 francs debt; but then, 'I am neither frugal nor
prodigal ... I have often meditated on what standard is just
fitting to keep up appearances, and that's what has rescued me

most often from difficulties, as I've gained a lot of skill in ways and means of putting up a good show.' The others, who had not studied the problem with such insight, but erred on the side of prodigality, found that they too must concentrate on their finances. Absentee landlords, with little interest in agricultural improvement ('Whenever you stumble on a *grand seigneur*', says Arthur Young, 'even one that was worth millions, you are sure to find his property desert'), they were yet anxious to get the last ounce of profit out of their lands, and the steady price rise up to 1775 helped them to sell grain and wine and wood at advantageous rates. It is their insistence on their income which accounts for the feudal reaction at the end of the old régime, the pressure for arrears of ancient dues, the revival of old rights, and the appointment of professional feudists to redraw terriers on the iniquitous basis of payment by results. In Anjou, the *seigneurs haut justiciers* were claiming the very roadside trees. Money derived from their estates was often invested in large-scale commercial and industrial ventures. The social upheaval of Law's scheme and alliances with the financiers had removed the inhibitions of the court nobility, some of the great names of France being concerned with investments in the mines of Flanders and in the lucrative sugar and coffee trade with San Domingo. In Franche-Comté, forge masters were acting as agents for the comte de Rosen, the prince de Montbéliard, the comte d'Autrey, the comte de Vercel, the duc de Randan and the prince de Bauffrement, and in the king's duchy of Châteauroux the comte d'Esseville was intriguing for the concession of the ironworks in 1771. Then there were less reputable activities of profit-making; the duc de Montmorency Luxembourg, whose servants' wages were fantastically in arrears, in 1789 had over half a million loaned out, and in the reign of Louis XV the prince de Carignan and M. de Gesvres were drawing 120,000 l. a year each from the roulette tables in the gaming house they ran at Paris. The Orléans family, at once more thick-skinned and more enterprising than the rest, recouped its broken fortunes by throwing open the Palais-Royal and renting out stalls on the premises to booksellers, wig-makers and lemonade vendors.

For younger sons especially, the Church could serve as a system of luxurious outdoor relief. The Order of Malta and the orders of lay canonesses were by now lay sinecures with little that was genuinely ecclesiastical about their purpose. Abbeys were held in *commendam* by courtiers whose only sacrifice to the rules of the Church had been a lock of hair when they were tonsured at the age of seven; such a one was prince Louis de Bourbon Condé, drawing 400,000 l. a year as titular abbot of four monasteries, who made his nearest approach to the performance of an abbatial function when he built a marble tomb for his pet monkey McCarthy. There had been a few non-noble bishops at the end of the reign of Louis XIV, there were none at all in 1789. Read the correspondence of Mme de Sévigné about a bishopric for her nephew, or of Bernis to Choiseul on a similar topic, and all you hear of is the amount of the revenue, the agreeable house, its handiness for Paris, the value of this 'stepping stone' to a better see. The aristocracy brought into the episcopate their characteristic vices, luxury, non-residence, worldliness, which they would excuse on the sort of grounds Archbishop Dillon appealed to when explaining to Louis XVI why he prohibited the chase to his clergy yet hunted furiously himself – 'Sire, my clergy's vices are their own, mine come from my ancestry.' On the other hand, they brought the characteristic virtues of their race, sometimes a great devotion to duty and a lofty piety, more often a proud inflexible independence, and above all, great administrative skill, which produced the special class of 'administrative bishops' at the end of the old régime, great educators, cutters of canals, builders and planners, open-handed and charitable. Boisgelin, Champion de Cicé and Loménie de Brienne (and Turgot might easily have been of their number) were men whose theological beliefs disqualify them for praise as prelates, but they qualify at least as the more useful members of the aristocracy.

Not all the bishops were non-resident, and in considering

the episcopate we have already moved from the high society of the capital towards the social life of the provinces. The gilded nobility of the court were not often seen on their distant estates. An apartment at Versailles, a magnificent *hôtel* in Paris and a country house near by were the standard fashionable dwellings required by the great, while the feudal keep of their ancestors crumbled away forgotten. Yet not all were strangers to provincial life. That sober general and industrialist, the duc de Croy, in spite of his inevitable residences in Paris and at court, his country house at Ivry-sur-Seine and his pleasant hill-top observatory at Châtillon, yet loved best of all his native town of Condé, 'the cradle of our race and very precious' – the centre too of his vast coal-mining and cotton-spinning investments. Here he interested himself in canals and improvements, in plans for a new parish church, in the extension of his domains, and, over twenty years and at a cost of a quarter of a million, he built a mansion which quite eclipsed the family *château* in the town. But the local interests of the duc de Croy the industrialist, like those of the duc de Liancourt the agriculturalist, were exceptional, and it is to other strata of the nobility that we must turn when we consider the structure of society in the provinces. Here the regional diversity of French life in the eighteenth century imposes continual qualifications on any generalization one may make concerning the nobility. The relation of nobles to peasantry is not likely to be the same in Burgundy, Picardy, Artois and Béarn, where the former class owned a quarter to a third of the land, as it is in Dauphiné, Quercy and Limousin, where it owned little more than a tenth. Great landholders with their property in solid blocks, with woods where the expensive timber for fencing could easily be obtained, and producing for sale in the open market, are found as the promovers and apologists of the enclosure movement of the second half of the century. On the other hand, the hunting rights of the nobles around Lyon, rents levied from the peasants for the use of the common pasture in the central provinces and Dauphiné, and the preferential grazing rights

of the lord of the manor in Lorraine and Béarn were enough
to turn the nobility of these areas into strong opponents of
enclosure, and bring them into an odd alliance with the cause
of the landless peasant. This example from the realm of economic circumstances could be matched by others taken from
the sphere of traditions and loyalties and honorary distinctions.
Within a framework of national law, customary law and feudal
vagaries French provincial life circled round intendants, bishops,
military governors, parlements, municipalities, landowners,
feudal superiors, and endless officials in a bewildering complexity, which is a living historical growth defying mere analysis.

Amid the infinite diversity of provincial life there is one
class of the nobility which, it is true, can easily be isolated for
separate study, that is, the magistrates of the eleven provincial
parlements and of the corresponding courts of Alsace and
Roussillon. Even so, they were not a united body following
the lead of the Parlement of Paris. Their union with Paris in
opposition to the royal power, generally dated from the years
1754-5, was essentially a union of local aristocracies, driven
into league as a reaction of auto-defence. Politically, their
claims to be the heirs of the old provincial councils accorded
ill with the claim of the Parlement of Paris to succeed the
national assemblies of the Germanic period. There is many a
rift on the question of the expulsion of the Jesuits, while on
the physiocratic issue of freeing the corn trade and on the
recurrent problem of national bankruptcy there is a divergence
of policy between the rentiers of Paris and the landowners of
the provinces. A leading magistrate of the Parlement of Nor-
mandy writes in 1771, 'The connections between the parlements are rare . . . for the provincial parlements are always
discontented with the tone of superiority of that of Paris . . .
each thinks that it is at least the equal and often the superior of
its neighbours by the date of its foundation, so that they only
have to write to each other to set themselves by the ears.' So if
we study them as a university, we must make allowances for
the collegiate system.

These local aristocracies, once a middle term between nobility and bourgeoisie, have now become closed castes themselves. Four quarters of nobility were required to enter, even when there was no official ruling to this effect, as at Dijon, where in 1789 only one commoner was a magistrate of the Parlement of Burgundy, and a hundred of the one hundred and twenty had entered upon their offices before the age of twenty. Minor dynasties, like the d'Ormessons, the Joly de Fleurys, the Molés and the d'Aguesseaus of Paris had formed in the provinces, hereditary families of the robe, of great local distinction. 'Elle a refusé des Présidents à mortier, c'est tout dire', said Mme de Sévigné of an eligible but difficult young lady. They were rich (except in Brittany), and, unlike the gilded nobility of the court, they were not spendthrift. Their money invariably went into real property. At Dijon, there is only one subscriber to the Company of the Indies, but there are many owners of mills, slate-quarries, ironworks, and above all of domains and vineyards under constant improvement, with many records of new purchases of land, and not a single trace of its sale. The wealthy magistrates regarded themselves as in no way inferior to the nobles who owed their origin to the sword; 'the unanimity of sentiments directed towards honour and virtue', says the Parlement of Grenoble in 1756, 'makes both these nobilities from henceforward one single body'. On the other hand, the old nobility of a strong military tradition did not disdain the distinction of a career in the robe; the baron de Gaix wrote in his testament of 1781 to his three sons, 'Vous avez à choisir entre la robe et le service'. 'The first of these two states', he added 'is no less respectable than the second.' Yet all the while, under the surface, their rivalry remained, to manifest itself continually on points of punctilio and precedence. In particular, the older nobility envied the political rôle that the lawyers were assuming, and one of the factors which one must take into account in the strange complex of upper-class aspirations and jealousies which expresses itself in the demand for provincial estates in the last years of the old régime is this split between magistrature and the rest of the nobility, the former swinging against the movement in proportion as the others adhere to it.

In the provinces, parlements and bishops, and the great nobles holding titular military offices, were all alike overshadowed by one powerful agent of the central government, the intendant. De Tocqueville's picture of a stranger to the province, a man of non-noble birth, with his way in the world to make, is wrong at every point, so far as the eighteenth century is concerned. The intendants were nobles of parliamentary families, with strong local connections, with their great position in life ready made for them. They were, in fact, recruited from the eighty *maîtres des requêtes*, an inner ring of administrative magistrates which had arisen within the judicial magistracy. 'The parlements', says Ardescheff, 'were the antechamber of the intendancy.' This administrative magistracy was, in its turn, becoming a closed caste, as we may see from the fact that, of Louis XVI's intendants, fourteen are sons of intendants, often appointed at a very early age, and in some cases inheriting directly from their fathers. Money again was the determining factor in the social hierarchy. The *conseiller* of parlement had purchased his office, wealth then brought his descendants to the office of *maître des requêtes*, wealth again was taken into consideration by the government when appointing to the expensive post of intendant. A few were of the old feudal nobility, though these had penetrated through the ranks of the magistrature, a few nobles whose origin does not go beyond the third generation, but the vast majority were 'ancienne noblesse', that is, those who would not qualify for the test of presentation at court, but who passed the normal test of four quarters. In other words, just the right number of generations for a family to buy its way through the appropriate offices.

There remain the unlucky branches of the nobility – it goes without saying that we find them in the provinces – which remained poor. Not all were desperately so, for poverty has its hierarchy as well as riches, and different families and different branches enjoyed varying prosperity according to the vagaries of the inheritance laws in various provinces and the enterprise of individuals. The nobles of Anjou were penurious enough, yet Walsh, comte de Serrant, their natural leader, stood on the fringe of the court nobility, and could entertain royally the sister of Marie-Antoinette or the ambassadors of Tippo Sahib. Further down the scale came a comte de Montlosier, directing, somewhat aloofly, the agricultural improvements on his estate near Clermont, which boasted forty head of cattle and five hundred sheep. A profitable alternation between army and church might very successfully provide for a large family; a noble of an old family like René-Gilbert Anne, chevalier de la Corbière had his eldest son a colonel, two other sons officers who met their deaths in the wars, one son archdeacon in the cathedral at Vannes and another a canon of Luçon. There was a whole proletariat of sunken nobles in Brittany, yet Chateaubriand's father, who had somewhat restored the family fortune by adventuring beyond seas, could live in the château of Comburg with his modest retinue of five servants, a hunting dog and two old mares, spending his time in his study in the west tower with a genealogical tree above the fireplace, in the vast *salon* by the light of a single candle, or on the terrace after supper, brooding, and shooting the occasional owl. But, below all these, there was a poverty-stricken mass of country gentry. Such were the squires of Beauce who, as the proverb had it, stayed in bed while their breeches were mended, the nobles around Auch whom Arthur Young found ploughing their own fields, the home-spun aristocrats of Poitou whose daughters kept the flocks, the Breton gentry who went to market with a sword on one side and a basket on the other. How could this hard-up nobility exist? The files of the central government and of the intendants were full of their appeals for favours, to get their daughters into convents, their sons into seminaries or the army. Their tragedy was that pride prevented them from striking out into commerce, the resource, as Voltaire observed with admiration, of younger sons in England. The opportunity was there, for the so-called *loi de dérogeance* had never applied universally, and government policy, more especially after the storm raised by the abbé Coyer in 1756, was directed to encouraging the nobility to take part in trade. But these poverty-stricken provincial families were unyielding. It was the gilded nobility who were able to overcome their inhibitions, illustrating yet another trait of a society ruled by money – that big financial transactions are always respectable, only the petty juggling with money being mercenary.

The one remaining resource for the poor nobility was the army, and here the court nobility had the virtual monopoly of the higher commands, and the plutocracy was infiltrating from below by buying commissions. There were various attempts to limit commissions to those of noble birth, in particular by the comte de St.-Germain, himself a poor noble who had to rise to eminence in foreign service before gaining high rank in France. These were not signs of a feudal reaction, but were rather the last efforts of the poorer nobility to preserve its sole profession from the invading power of money. It was among the impecunious provincial families that the military tradition which was the original justification for the existence of their order remained alive. Whenever war broke out, they rallied to the standards, seeking, said Voltaire sardonically and uncomprehendingly, the brevet of lieutenant which was their passport to death.

There was then no reason why they should admit, and they never would admit, to being inferior to the gilded nobility of the court. For them the only tests within the order were lineage, or service to the state. Their cahiers put this clearly. The nobles of Arras say, 'The nobility of France is a body which is essentially indivisible'; those of Évreux object to the words 'première noblesse' in a recent edict – 'this expression tends to divide an order in which the general title of every individual composing it is that of *gentilhomme*.' They are protesting against the chief reality in the social life of their day, the power of money. The French nobility is severed completely between rich and poor, yet, quite rightly, they are insisting that if there is to be a nobility at all, this gulf is illogical. The significance of this social situation is revealed in 1789. In April, Malouet, the cardinal de La Luzerne and the reforming comte d'Antraigues suggested a Second Chamber, and on 31st August Lally and Clermont-Tonnerre put forward the idea in the Assembly. Just as the aristocratic monopoly of bishoprics and great benefices had prevented the order of the Clergy from opposing the march of revolutionary events, so now a similar split was revealed in the second order in the state, for the idea of a Second Chamber received no support from the provincial nobility, who knew too well who were meant to sit in the new senate. United by the exemptions of privilege and the distinctions of pride which aroused against them the intelligent middle orders of the nation, who envied but could not infiltrate, the nobility was nevertheless completely divided on the scale of riches and poverty. Envied, but disunited, they were doomed to political ineffectiveness.

The mention of privilege brings us to another rift in the nobility, a paradoxical contrast between the development of their ideas and their actual position in society, between their growing addiction to plans of reform, and the whole structure of abuses which served their interests. One of the roots of this movement of thought was spiritual. A society which had become 'too civilized', which, as two acute feminine observers, Mme de Staël and Mme de Genlis both agree, had come to live only for vanity, had reached the term of its introverted existence. The growing attraction of freemasonry, the furore of occultism in Paris in the 'eighties, the vogue of Rousseauistic sensibility, reveal a search for a religion of humanity to replace the dying confessional beliefs of a social world which now went to mass only to impress its lackeys. Here, inevitably, are the implications of a theoretical egalitarianism, for when man is the measure, men must be equal. 'The man I esteem the most is the most honest man, without asking what his birth is', said the maréchal de Castéja, rebuking a snobbish land agent, who refused to eat with the servants. But this hit, palpable as it is, by a noble of the old régime against Babeuf, the future egalitarian conspirator, represents only one aspect of the reforming movement among the French nobility. It would be a naïve view which regarded them as blindly and light-heartedly toying with doctrines which were ultimately to mean their ruin, the view of the vicomtesse de Noailles that 'in the end, like the astrologer in the fable, we fell into a well when we were looking up at the stars'. The *émigrés*, in haunted penitence, were wont to magnify their miscalculations into apostasies. Quixotic and reckless acceptance of levelling doctrines is less than half the story, for there was a continuous trend of reforming thought throughout the eighteenth century which sought to refound the state upon the aristocracy. Fénélon dreamt of a revived and purified nobility leading the nation; from Montesquieu came the view that the privileged class formed the essential middle term which alone could prevent a monarchy degenerating into a despotism. There is an undertone of thought which may be best described as feudal, becoming articulate in the yearnings of Boulainvilliers for the free aristocratic leadership of the age of the Frankish conquerors, and the rage of the marquis de Mirabeau at the royal encroachments; there is the desire for the revival of the military caste, exemplified in the writings of the chevalier d'Arc and in the highly personal, almost existential cult of 'glory' in Vauvenargues, and, more prosaically, in the government's rehabilitation of the Corsican nobility in the military academies of France. Above all (for there is no time to pause over the circumstances which made the future refounder of the aristocracy a cadet at Brienne), there was the ever-present example of England, where the great lords ran the country. Constitutional Anglomania was not the result of ignorance concerning the real nature of the government of England, for French publicists made the most of rotten boroughs and electoral manipulations. On the contrary, Rabaud Saint-Étienne's condemnation of a system where 'nation and

king would be nothing, the aristocrats would be everything'
was precisely descriptive of the attraction. Archbishop Boisgelin yearned for the opportunities of Fox, who 'commanded
his nation and his sovereign', and Ségur declares that 'the
brilliant but frivolous life of our nobility, at court and in town,
could no longer satisfy our pride, when we thought of the
dignity and independence of a peer of England, of a member
of the House of Commons'. True, a more democratic wind
blows in from America, but one must remember the many
cross-currents in the enthusiasm, the basic desire for revenge
upon England, the quest for glory of officers who re-embarked
when Congress would not create them generals, the plot of
the maréchal de Broglie who hoped to be stadtholder of the
independent colonies. The enthusiasms of the French nobility
were yoked in harness with their ambitions.

It was unfortunate that the reform movement among the
nobility found no adequate rallying point. There were two
available traditions of resistance to the crown; on the issues of
Jansenism and finance the Parlement of Paris had developed a
claim to represent the nation, while the Orleanist movement
was a tradition of opposition centring in an unemployed family
of the blood royal. But the parlements could only claim to
represent the nation when no other mouthpiece of public
opinion was available, and the hardening of caste barriers in the
magistrature and the rapid decline in the value of judicial office
throughout the century revealed that even as a mechanism for
taking new generations of wealth into mesh with the driving
wheel of state their usefulness was worn out. On the other
hand, the Orleanist movement provided just the kind of
leadership which brought out the worst qualities of the great;
it was a shabby Fronde springing from the ambitions of courtiers, aristocratic Anglomania and hatred of Marie-Antoinette,
and supplied with a dash of ideas and organization by Mme de
Genlis and Choderlos de Laclos. Nevertheless, it was around
these two traditions that the liberal nobility at first organized.
In defence of the parlements the *Comité des Trente* was formed,

in the Orleanist *salons* the clubland of liberalism foregathered, and from these groups comes the demand for a constitution, the move of a minority to join the Third Estate, and the plan of renunciation of 4th August.

The constitutional and liberal movement among the French aristocracy was largely confined to the high society of the capital, where distinctions of wealth were replacing those of birth, and a temper of thought had arisen which corresponded to the new social structure. It was here that the nobility glimpsed the possible nature of the new order, and were playing their cards to obtain its leadership, if necessary, in alliance with the plutocracy. In the country at large, the rest of the nobility were not so clear-sighted, nor did they have the opportunity and financial power. Their *cahiers* show that they were for individual liberty, toleration, a constitution, and, in many cases, were willing to relinquish their financial exemptions. But they were adamant on the question of vote by order; that is, they were willing to relinquish privilege and honorary distinction, except where such privilege and distinction involved the reality of political power. They too had their political ambition, but they had not the willingness of the young men in the capital to launch out boldly into a society where money would avowedly count for more than birth.

It is the business of the historian, said Napoleon, to carve the past at the joints, and in this lecture we have chosen the scale of wealth as our diagram of dissection. Of course, no one system of classification could ever be satisfactory when we are trying to classify living human beings. Talleyrand the ordinand taking a young actress home from the church of St.-Sulpice under his umbrella; bishop du Tillet wandering round the cottages of his diocese, dog at heels and pastoral staff in hand; Choderlos de Laclos the hard-up artillery officer writing the novel that anticipates the technique of Stendhal; the old duc de Villars with painted eyebrows and padded cheeks; the ne'er-do-well M. de Louvois who had his clothes tailored from the family tapestry; Louis d'Orléans and the gay duchesse de

Bourbon forsaking the world and giving their immense wealth to the poor; the maréchal de Noailles creeping under a shroud to have the offices of the dead read over him; the duchesse de Luynes counting the rigorous days of Lent; Mme de Chalais seated on her high velvet chair in the dispensary supervising the treatment of the sick; the duc d'Olonne robbing tradesmen by main force until a *lettre de cachet* ends the career of ducal shoplifting; the président de Piolance hobnobbing in the parliamentary vacation with the smuggler Mandarin; the sordid marquis de Sade; the marquis de St.-Huruge who leads workers' risings in the *faubourg St.-Antoine*; Mirabeau writing pamphlets to rig the stock-exchange; the prince de Montbarey wounded in battle at the age of twelve with his tutor by his side; the comte de Sabran fighting the English off Gibraltar, receiving eleven wounds, and when shot runs out, charging the cannon with his table silver; Chassé, the famous bass of the Opera, ennobled by royal favour, to the astonishment of the good *avocat* in Brittany who was his brother – no classification can be adequate for such people. Whatever their virtues and vices, they have one trait in common: proud, self-confident independence. They cannot be subsumed under the facile heading of a class. They are self-consciously individual, they are themselves. So, in considering briefly the French nobility of the eighteenth century, one can only seize on some principle of division which seems to be the most significant, and in choosing the scale of wealth, one at least explains the inner contradictions of the order, and accounts for its ineffectiveness in the march of revolutionary events. In exile, they elaborated theories of the causes of those events based on mysticism, masonry, divine vengeance or levelling philosophy, theories which are the unconscious excuses of a class to cover the real facts about their decline. As it is Arthur Young records their divided weakness – 'Fortunately for France, they fall without a struggle, and die without a blow'.

3

SPAIN

Raymond Carr

THE nobility of Spain was given its formal structure when Charles I divided the vague, undifferentiated, mediaeval nobility into three classes. At the top of the hierarchy came the old 'rich men of Castille', the great magnates who now became grandees of Spain. Grandeeship was a distinction independent of any other title: its holder might be a duke like Alba or a count like Lemos. Within the circle of the grandees all are equal. Beneath the grandees came the titled nobility (*títulos*) – dukes, marquesses and counts. At the base were the untitled *hidalgos*.

The division of Charles I did not create the nobility of the great families: it merely recognized a pre-eminence given to them by history. The king could neglect the just claims of the 'injured houses' to grandeeships: the grandees underlined royal error by treating the aggrieved as their social equals. It is this historic origin of greatness, independent of royal grant, that explains the position of the score of old families who claimed to be the equals of the French princes of the blood. Their claims were put to Philip V by Arcos and Lemos. 'His Majesty is free to make whom he chooses cover in his presence but the grandeeship of the Counts of Lemos was made by God and time.'

This exclusive pride suffered under Philip V. There were isolated humiliations – Medina Celi's imprisonment, Arcos' enforced calls on the French princes of the blood. Lavish creation – Philip created as many grandees as were created in the whole

seventeenth century – together with a neglect of those ceremonial distinctions that had preserved the special position of
the immemorial grandees were intended to weaken the caste.
Exclusiveness could only assert itself by withholding *tu* from
newcomers to greatness, and it is curious to observe Charles III
persuading the grandees to use this familiar form of his greatest
personal friend, Losada. In spite of Philip's attack, the core of
old families remained a caste apart in the grandeeship: *la voz
antigua de la sangre* was irresistible when its sounding-board was
great possessions which no newcomer could hope to match.

Parallel with the extension of the grandees was the extension
of the titled nobility. Here, again, Philip V's reign was the crisis;
he created over half the titled nobility of the eighteenth century.
His successors were more sparing. They rewarded service
rather than mere loyalty to the new dynasty, though the services
rewarded were often of a trifling nature – a fact which manifested
itself in titles like the Marquessate of Royal Transport and of the
Guarantee. Mere title in itself was no indication of social status
or local influence: already by the end of the century satirists
are commenting that there was scarcely a river, village, or field
of Spain that had not a title attached to it. Since the upper
ranges of the titled were absorbed into the grandeeship, the
titled nobility tended to consist of a remnant of obscure, if
ancient, provincial families who had never made their names
at court, together with newly ennobled government servants.

At the base of the hierarchy the *hidalgo*, like the immemorial
grandee, could claim that history rather than royal creation
was the basis of his nobility. Whole provinces in the north
could claim *hidalgúia* as a relic of participation in the reconquest.
Apart from these general claims, the combined workings of
afán de nobleza and royal poverty had swollen the *hidalgo* class
to include those without land or the jurisdictional rights of
señorio. The poor *hidalgo* was neither a squire nor a provincial
aristocrat. The census of 1787 shows how violently the social
content of the word *hidalgo* could vary from province to
province. In the Basque provinces it comprised the whole

male population; in the south and centre under 1 per cent.

Thus, of the half million nobles of the census of 1787, only the grandees, the greater titled nobility and the few *hidalgos* with sizeable estates can be classed with the continental nobility. A French observer commented on the weakening of the conception of nobility through over-extension: *si tous les hommes étaient de la même taille les mots de géans et de nains seraient rayés de tous les dictionnaires.*

What part did this aristocracy play in the political life of Spain? From the days of the Catholic kings the history of the Spanish aristocracy has been regarded as one of increasing political impotence, on the assumption that an aristocracy is powerless once it has gone to court. In fact the seventeenth century saw a recovery of aristocratic power at the expense of a feeble crown. A court aristocracy has its own weapons: the court strike that failed to intimidate Olivares; intrigue with malcontents in the royal house which did succeed in driving from power Valenzuela, the son of a captain from Ronda. If these plotters had been men of even moderate industry and ability, they might have retained power. Unfortunately for them they justified Olivares' verdict. *A todo los tenía por inutiles.*

Louville echoed Olivares. *Les grands sont tous des imbéciles, bas, sans force ni vertu.* Yet neither Louis XIV nor Philip V dismissed lightly the opposition of the higher aristocracy to the new dynasty. The strength of this opposition, in spite of the weakening forces of absenteeism, lay in the social power of the aristocracy in the localities. Amelot, like Olivares before him but with less reason, feared the aristocracy as leaders of provincial revolt. *Ils pourraient être plus dangereux parmi leurs vassaux qu'à la cour.* An historic memory of the separatist nobility of Aragon, Andalusia and Portugal still haunted the architect of a centralized monarchy on the French pattern, so unpleasing to nobles who had enjoyed the benefits of the Austrian lack of governance.

Local power was rooted in the part played by the aristocracy in municipal government and in the judicial rights of *señorio*.

Inferior though seignorial justice might be, Patiño recognized in it the secret of the Catalonian rebel barons' hold over the countryside. All over Spain this hold had grown in the seventeenth century when the crown had sold municipal office and rights of *señorio*. By 1787, though the great cities were usually 'royal', the smaller towns were predominantly seignorial and the smaller units dominated by the great aristocracy in certain districts (e.g. León, Andalusia, Galicia). Municipal office continued to be the characteristic activity of the provincial nobility until well into the nineteenth century.

The greatest single blow suffered by the aristocracy in the eighteenth century was the abolition of their exceptional jurisdictions in Aragon, as a punishment for rebellion and in the interests of uniformity. Apart from this little came of the efforts of reformers to buy back, or at least effectively supervise, these private jurisdictions. Not till 1811 did a series of laws whittle away the nobles' seignorial jurisdictions, thus destroying some of their connection with the localities. This, rather than any financial loss through an act of sheer expropriation, was the significance of liberal reform.

The civil war of the Spanish Succession showed that the loyalty of the grandees to the dynasty was often lukewarm and interested when it was not actually suspect. Apart from genuine ties to the old dynasty – Leganez refused to 'draw the sword against the house of Austria to whom my own house owes so many benefits' – it could not be expected that the grandees would welcome the centralizing reforms of the new dynasty. Tessé, with some exaggeration, called them the only Spanish enemies of the dynasty; Louville, *fidèles par lâcheté et par intérêt*. Apart from the spectacular treasons of Legánez and Cabrera, even the more favourably inclined, according to Louis XIV himself, did not care who won – and they showed their indifference by retiring to their estates to await events in the monarchy's greatest hour of need (1705–6).

The mutual suspicions of the higher aristocracy and the dynasty meant that political power could not, in the early years, be entrusted with safety to the grandees; the experiment with the proud, ambitious Medina Celi was not encouraging and his fall and imprisonment was a blow to his whole caste. The dynasty could, and did, find loyal servants of pedestrian quality; but even the loyal were confined to court office where a tedious ceremonial emphasized that subject and sovereign were clean different things. Real power lay elsewhere with the king's immediate advisers – in the early years French administrative experts like Amelot and Orry, foreigners like Alberoni whom Bubb Doddington found to be 'the gentleman who is alone absolute here'.

As the century progressed and the dynasty strengthened, this purely political suspicion weakened. Charles III was not anti-aristocratic – the aristocracy did not throw up the kind of servants that an autocrat could use. The dynasty found its servants either in Italians (Grimaldi and Esquilache) or in native Spanish administrators – great civil servants of relatively humble birth of the type of Patiño and Floridablanca. The Council of Castille, the administrative centre of the monarchy, was almost the exclusive preserve of professional jurists who had made a career in the provincial *audiencias* and chancelleries. Apart from the Paris embassy – always given to a grandee – the old nobility did not by any means monopolize the diplomatic service, still less the American administration. The higher ranges of the church had never been a noble preserve – an eighteenth-century Primate was the son of a Gibraltarian charcoal burner. The letters of Fernán-Nuñez show that even the army, in spite of Charles III's efforts, was scarcely a satisfactory career for the young aristocrat in the time of O'Reilly. The only pasture left was court office with the reward of an *encomienda* in one of the military orders. Any ground recaptured in the seventeenth century was irretrievably lost to the professional servants of an absolute king, or to court favourites. Godoy, son of an Andalusian *hidalgo*, was everything that the grandees detested.

This dependence on professional administrators – the *golillas*

– did not pass without protest. The grandees, as in the days of Valenzuela's power, allied with the heir apparent against the king and his low-born counsellors so that the *Cuarto del Principe* becomes a pale imitation of Leicester House. In Charles III's time Aranda, a rich, ill-tempered, boorish Aragonese magnate, formed a party of malcontents including the ambitious Villahermosa and some of his Pignatelli connections, a party which could boast the support of the Prince of the Asturias. But Aranda could not force himself to power. His 'independence', although it saved the monarchy in the riots of 1766, led him to insult the king to his face. He was a poor servant beside the industrious *golilla*. Finally, he came to power as a mere stopgap until María Luisa could push forward Godoy. Aranda was the only grandee who played an important part in eighteenth-century politics. But his whole career was an object-lesson that even an 'enlightened' aristocrat could not fit into the Bourbon monarchy as Charles III conceived it.

The strength of the higher nobility, and the pre-eminence of the old grandee families in particular, lay neither in their political influence nor in their seignorial jurisdictions, but in the sheer size of their estates; a contemporary estimate calculated that about a third of the cultivatable land of Spain was in the hands of four great houses. Even in the nineteenth century Greville, whose standard in these matters was no niggardly one, could quote with wonderment the income of a visiting grandee.

The legal institution which kept so large a proportion of the national wealth in the hands of the higher nobility was the Castillian *mayorazgo*, an imbarrable entail, which had grown up in the later Middle Ages. Lawyers' interpretations of the Laws of Toro (1505) consistently favoured the growth of entail and guarded its strict nature. It came to include moveables – the thirty pieces of silver for which Christ was betrayed, the amateur sketches of a San Esteban. It spread socially when the small entail (*mayorazgo corto*) 'democratized' the institution. It spread geographically to the non-Castillian provinces.

Strict entail, combined with an unusually frequent failure of male heirs, attributed by foreigners to aristocratic degeneracy, tended to agglomerate estates in the hands of the surviving grandees when marriage was restricted within the circle of grandee houses. The rich became richer, the titles acquired more titles when sole heiresses took their lands and titles with them. This process affected almost every great house (e.g. Medina Sidonia titles and lands to the husband of sole heiress of Alba; Infantado *via* Tavara to Osuna; Béjar *via* niece to Osuna). Any restrictions put in the way of such amalgamations by legislation or the technical incompatibility of different estates were eluded by legal and heraldic fictions. By the end of the eighteenth century the *Informe* of Guerra y Sandoval shows that every great house held incompatible entails.

The main onslaught on the great entailed estates came from the reformers in the government, although many aristocrats were aware of the inconveniences of strict entail, e.g. difficulties with marriage settlements for *segundones* who would not inherit, mortgages, etc. The consistent criticisms of the reformers became the polemical arsenal for later, often misguided, left-wing attacks on the *latifundia*. The great entailed *latifundia* were to be found in Andalusia, southern Castille, Estremadura, La Mancha and parts of Aragon; they were localized phenomena but of the greatest importance to us, because it was from these *latifundia*, combined with extensive holdings of a different type in Galicia, León and Old Castille, that the great aristocracy drew the bulk of its income.

Most of the real and supposed evils of the great estates were connected with absenteeism. This social habit has been misinterpreted. The great southern and Galician nobles were absentees in the sense that they lived 'at the Court'; when, in disgrace at Court, they condescended to visit their estates, it was an event never forgotten by the subjects, who fêted the *señor* as a provincial town fêtes visiting royalty, with loyal addresses, and processions and church services. But the nobility in general was not absentee in this extreme sense. It was urban.

Its chosen field of action was the closed municipal council with the opportunities office gave for the advantageous marketing of the products of their estates.

The Spanish aristocracy had no talent for a country life centred on the great house or the manor. There was no interest in field sports to attract them to the countryside: that was left to 'the greatest Nimrod of his time', Charles III, with whom the slaughter of game was an obsessive mania. 'They have not even the idea of gentlemen's country seats, with gardens about them', an English traveller noted. Their normal residence was the town house. These houses, with their coats of arms above the main door, can be seen in any provincial town. In Ronda they dominate the town, strung out high above the gorge.

Thus the Spanish aristocracy, with the exception of the northern provinces and parts of Catalonia, had little direct contact with its lands; it felt neither the economic advantages nor the social obligations of landholding. In the south, in particular, it was a purely urban, *rentier* class.

In such conditions it was vain to look for the improving landlord. Even when they were moved by the Physiocratic influences of the Economic Societies, the patriot thought more in terms of factories and schools than investment in his lands. This indifference, it was maintained, was but another consequence of the lawyers' devices which enabled entail to swallow all. Improvements went to the heir. Those with capital preferred to provide with it for their younger children; when income fell there was no thought of investment to improve returns, no possibility of sale to others. The estate collapsed. Thus the conservative defence of the entail and the large estate – then, as now, based on the assumption that only the rich landlord had the capital to bring the *secanos* into prosperity – was based on weak grounds. The Tarragona Economic Society, with the dusty estates of La Mancha in its mind's eye, dismissed the arguments of the political economists:

'They say that rich landowners can more easily buy good animals and afford the necessary instruments of cultivation, build dams, and irrigation canals ... works that the poor peasant, who has to fight in misery for his daily bread, can scarcely undertake. Yet let one of these economic gentlemen show us but one improvement made by a rich landowner. Where are their dams, their drains? How should those who spend their energies and capital on the luxuries of town life have time for such undertakings?' We can recognize here the moral flavour of the later nineteenth century attack on the *latifundia*.

It was not only that the landlords did not improve themselves: the reformers complained that the landed monopoly of the church and aristocracy combined with the communal pastures prevented others from improving by keeping land 'in slavery'. Entail allowed so little land into the market that its purchase price was too high to encourage investment (Jovellanos arbitrarily calculated the return as one-and-a-half per cent as compared with the six per cent to eight per cent in other forms of investment). Improving capitalists and peasant proprietors were alike starved of land. Olavide believed that 'He who buys, improves' and Jovellanos put his hopes in an enclosing race of peasant farmers moved by socially beneficent self-interest. The whole history of the nineteenth century proved both wrong: but the delusion that new forms of ownership would end the problems of dry farming (the great estates were for the most part in the *secano*) persisted.

In the entailed *latifundia* of the south, therefore, some land was leased at exorbitant rents on short leases to peasants who had no other incentive but to exhaust it. There can be little doubt that rents were rising rapidly in the eighteenth century. To stem this rise, reformers advocated a systematic extension of crop sharing to save the peasant in the 'years of hunger', or the substitution of fixed rents and long leases or emphyteutic tenures for the short lease. (Here the *mayorazgo* stood in the way of reform: the long lease was legally impossible for it prejudiced the interests of the heir.) When the lord cultivated his land directly through his steward it was worked with a seasonal labour force of immigrant reapers and chronically under-employed and under-paid *jornaleros* from the towns, then, as in the days of the Republic, the most miserable agrarian class in Europe. Beside these corn lands were the great *dehesas* – scrub pastures given over to bulls and sheep. Thus was produced the desolate landscape of the south; the widely separated agricultural towns, the open wheat-fields and vast pastures: '*Le grand propriétaire*', remarked Bourgoing, after he had ridden through the desert of Medina Sidonia's estates, '*semble y régner comme le lion dans les forêts, en éloignant par ses rugissements tout ce qui pourrait approcher de lui.*'

These conditions were common on the great estates of the centre and south, the economic foundation of the great nobility. Elsewhere conditions were often widely different. In the Basque provinces and Navarre tenure was secure and rack-renting by the provincial nobility a social impossibility. Wherever the *censo* (a quit-rent of two per cent with no eviction) prevailed, the landlord's grip on the land was weakened. Thus in Catalonia the social struggle of the Middle Ages had left a relatively prosperous *censo*-paying peasant class; the worst effects of the *mayorazgo* on leases were circumvented by a wide use of semi-legal emphyteutic tenures. Old Castille, parts of León and central Castille presented a different problem; estates tended to be small with the nobility resident in the neighbouring town. Here the *censo* could not emancipate the peasant and isolate the landlord. Already the landlords had begun their attempt to turn the *censo* into a short-term lease, pushing up the rent. All reports agree with the Castillian intendant who complained that the Castillian peasant was becoming 'a wretched slave'.

How much of the benefit of rising cereal prices and rising rents was passed on to the landlord? What were the effects of the acquired habits of the Spanish landholders on income?

All the evidence available would seem to show that the great southern landlords were insulated by a combination of distance, administrative practice and indifference, from the benefits of changing conditions. Only in Castille – and by the lesser nobility – was ruthless exploitation attempted for the immediate profit.

A desire not to be bothered with the running of their estates was the economic crime of the Spanish nobility. The economic indifference which made it a point of honour not to challenge bailiffs' accounts would be incredible were it not for constant reference to this peculiar form of aristocratic pride. Administrative ease led to the practice of renting large farms to middlemen, who kept the best land, rack-renting the marginal land: there is indisputable later evidence that this allowed the middlemen profits of five hundred per cent to nine hundred per cent – an emphatic proof of the disastrous economic consequences of ingrained habits of absenteeism. The *dehesas* in corn districts were another symptom of a preference for administrative ease to high profit at a time when it paid to cultivate marginal land, although it must be remembered that a terrible road system made marketing difficult. This was the most genuine economic hindrance to southern prosperity. Thus it would seem that only the size of their estates allowed the great nobility to survive as self-sufficing units, often with a high proportion of kind-rents, stored in the town house and which could be used, in a relatively primitive economy, to meet household expenses and part of the largest item of conspicuous waste – servants' wages.

Galicia is a separate case: but it tends to prove how, when great estates are let on emphyteutic tenures, profit eluded the owner of the *dominium directum*. The *foro* was a fixed quit-rent paid to the landowner, in Galicia usually a great noble or the church. In the eighteenth century a sharp rise in population created a demand for land which led the original *forero* (tenant) to sublet portions of his holding at enormous profit. Seeing the benefits of this process escape them, the landowners tried to call in the *foros* by enforcing a long-disused time limitation. In the subsequent legal struggle with the *foreros* the government sided against the landlords. They failed to become profiteers, they failed to become oppressors: this was left to the middle-men *foreros*, the standard-bearers of nineteenth century liberalism. The whole struggle proves how right the landlords were in their distaste for the emphyteutic tenures so dear to the reformers: the owner of the *dominium utile* showed a dangerous tendency to behave as if he were the owner of the *dominium directum*.

The attack of the reformers on the economic evils of the large estates failed in the eighteenth century; the *mayorazgo* was successfully defended as a social necessity, the foundation of aristocracy as such, much as Burke defended primogeniture. Legislation remedied some abuses: thus improvements were made compulsory on urban *mayorazgos*. Sale was made possible if the proceeds were invested in government loans (1795 and 1798) – these bond-holdings being in their turn inalienable family possessions. Cardenas maintains that the purpose of this legislation was 'to convert the whole entailed landed capital of Spain into holdings in the public debt'. That such a course could be proposed shows how much of an urban *rentier* class the aristocracy had become; it was a matter of indifference whether incomes came from land or government bonds.

The reforming tradition finally triumphed in the disentailing laws after 1820. Although the aristocracy often managed to keep their main estates by giving subsidiary urban property or liquid capital to the younger children, the legal protection of the great estate was gone for ever.

How did the Spanish aristocracy spend its income and live out its life?

Nobility consisted, for the most part, in the maintenance of the external characteristics of noble life. It was this fanatic pride in appearances which created that target of satirists and economists, the *hidalgúia proletaria*, the world of gentlemen beggars and odd-job men crowding the court and the houses of the great. Jovellanos maintained that those who could not live of their own should drop back into the working classes, a process he observed with approval in his native Asturias; but this was to go against the whole moral world of the poor *hidalgo* where laziness was the virtue that avoided the stigma of mechanic labour. 'How nourishing was the crust of black bread eaten beneath the genealogical tree.'

The most characteristically Spanish form of conspicuous waste demanded by 'position' was the maintenance of an eastern multitude of servants and clients – a private form of the *empleadismo* of the state. Arcos was commonly supposed to have retained 3000 dependents of various kinds when he died in 1780. This enormous *clientèle* accounts for the susceptibility of the Madrid mob to aristocratic influence in demonstrations against royal creatures. Wages and pensions often excluded other forms of expenditure – patronage of the arts or entertainment. The Spanish nobility had not that sumptuous garniture for its life usually associated with metropolitan aristocratic life. There were few great town houses in Madrid, few great collections of pictures if we exclude Alba, Medina Celi, Altamira and San Estebán.

A court aristocracy must take its tone from the court. The Spanish aristocracy had no independent civilization of its own to set beside the court. Apart from Ferdinand VI, none of the Spanish Bourbons gave consistent patronage to the arts. Charles III's standards may be judged by his unforgivable, hunting-squire insult to the greatest singer of his day. Moreover, his curious personal characteristics served only to intensify the mechanical precision of the gloomy, semi-conventual court life, with its mathematically timed migrations from royal residence to royal residence. Of these residences Bourgoing has left us his damning comment. '*Les résidences de la cour d'Espagne offrent peu de ressources du côté des plaisirs.*'

Nor did aristocratic society in general offer more. There traditional gloom was varied only by traditional frivolity – that world of social monotonies recreated in the novels of Pérez Galdos. In Madrid there was the deadening influence of the court; in the provinces, coach parades, 'low cards and dancing', the *maestranzas* – the social centres of the urban aristocracy devoted largely to the organization of bull-fights and the provision of pretty uniforms. It would be vain to look for a brilliant, cultured aristocracy. The universities were handed over to the career administrators; according to Cadalso, the formative years of the *señorito* were spent among household servants, stable-hands and local worthies like the cigar-making butcher, Tio Gregorio. In the barren early years of the century it is surprising enough to find educated men like Béjar and Alba, both pupils of Juan de Iriarte, or to come across the *salon* of the Countess of Lemos, where Luzán preached the doctrines of neo-classicism.

It was towards the middle of the century that a change came over the social and intellectual life of the best of the Spanish aristocracy. The impulse came from abroad. The Family Alliance enforced contact with France. The habit of sending young nobles to be educated abroad – especially to the Jesuit College of Sorèze – grew with the idea of the grand tour. There was an influential, though small, semi-permanent Spanish colony centred round the Paris embassy. It included at one time the Infantados, Santa Cruz, Priego, Fernán-Nuñez and the young Marquess of Mora, lover of Mlle de Lespinasse and correspondent of d'Alembert.

In Spain these new, hopeful currents found their natural medium of expression in the Patriotic Economic Societies. In spite of artificial injections of enthusiasm by the government, in spite of their amateurish scientific culture and the pompous phraseology adopted at childish prize-giving ceremonies, these societies did provide an outlet for the energies of the provincial nobility. 'This class of vassals', wrote an enthusiast for the societies, 'considered themselves excluded from contributing to the happiness of the kingdom outside the narrow limits of their own estates or through participation in municipal office in their local town.' Now this forced inactivity was over: they could enter *la gerarquia del gobierno*. Indeed the writer seems to have regarded the societies as the chosen instruments for a nascent aristocratic constitutionalism: as provincial deputations where the nobility could fulfil its traditional function of mediating between the king and his subjects.

Peñaflorida was a typical representative of the best aspects of this movement in the north. Rich, by Basque standards, he had been educated at Toulouse, where he formed an interest for science and music – the latter leading him to the typically vain liberal endeavour of substituting comic opera for bull-fighting. Mayor of his home town, he used his influence to turn the evening *tertulia* into an academy debating different topics each night of the week. Much of his scientific knowledge was amateurish – but so was Voltaire's – yet there is genuine enthusiasm behind his collection of electrical machines from Paris, microscopes from London, and in the formulation of a plan of agricultural reform based on an odd copy of the proceedings of the Dublin Society. When the Academy of Azcoita languished, Peñaflorida became the moving spirit of the new Royal Society of the Basque Provinces. His whole energy went into the foundation of a modern school in Vergara. Leaving his native town to be near the school, he became its first director. It was not an ignoble nor a wasted career.

It has always been difficult to estimate the strength of these new influences, to calculate depth as opposed to superficial extension. In particular, the nature of the influence of French rationalist thought has been hotly debated. The issues involved are still relevant. The traditionalists in modern Spain see in this influence the corrosion of alien thought, whereas the reforming tradition condones and even praises it as one of the by-products of a new Spain.

The free thinking of Aranda, Azara and Olavide was clearly exceptional. Most of those nobles who were confronted with radical French thinkers preferred flirtation to the marriage of true minds. Villahermosa listened to the sickening flattery of Voltaire without a change of heart; the Infantados maintained an essentially Spanish life in Paris itself. The last wish of Fernán-Nuñez, who passed as an *esprit fort*, was to go to Rome to seek the Pope's blessing. It was easy enough to pose as a *philosophe* in Paris; but there was little support in Madrid society for free thinking.

When every allowance has been made for the shallowness of the new influence, even when we remember the brutal ignorance of many of the grandees – that favourite topic of foreign observers – there can be little doubt that the nobility on the eve of the French Revolution contained men who were more travelled and better educated than their fathers.

There is something symbolic about the Marquess of Santa Cruz startling his neighbours by sending up a fire balloon from his garden. The innovation lay not in the scientific principles involved, for they were a direct importation from Paris, but in the fact that such principles were being demonstrated in Madrid. Too much emphasis on the second-hand nature of the new movement can obscure its importance to Spain. As might have been expected, the show-piece of the Spanish enlightenment, Aranda the hammer of the Jesuits, cut a poor figure in Paris society with his comical French and his bizarre ideas of his own importance. Aranda's career has sometimes been judged as if his poor performance in the *salons* of Paris, whence he derived his ideas, was of more importance than his influence in Madrid, where he propagated them.

These influences from abroad were beginning to loosen social life itself. Even in Córdoba Clarke seems to have found a passable social life. There can be little doubt that the Madrid of Charles IV and Marie-Louise, with all its faults, was a pleasanter society than the court of the 'good old king'. There were Godoy's receptions, where fawning grandees and women of evil report competed for the favours of the *valido*. However much the moral tone might shock the liberal priggery of Alcalá Galiano, it was an advance in civilization. There now was something that could be called society; a society that was riven by the rivalry of the Duchess of Alba, patroness of Goya, and the Countess-Duchess of Benavente – a rivalry that extended to competition for the patronage of Romero, the great artist of the *estocada a recibir*.

In spite of change the inherited forms of social intercourse still dominated social life. Thus, those foreign visitors who, by connection, could join as equals in the life of the Madrid aristocracy, felt themselves to be moving in a strange world, cut off from the amenities of civilized life. Few of the women could speak any language but Spanish and this added to the terrifying formality of the *tertulias* of the great – a French princess turned and fled at the door rather than face ordeal by conversation with a lady-in-waiting.

Two English visitors have left an account of high life at the end and turn of the century: William Eden, the ambassador, and Elizabeth, Lady Holland. To the latter, the normal forms of evening gathering, the *tertulia* or the less formal *rifresco*, were inexpressibly boring, with the sexes separated and no conversation. A Valencian ball was 'uncommonly dull'; 'what is called dancing is no more than jumping, leaping, jigging, walking, rolling, pacing, more or less in measure'. Eden's experiences of court life are almost moving in their dull agonies. 'I do not conceive it possible for any great city to be duller or less agreeable than Madrid; its cleanliness is its only virtue, in every other respect it is an execrable place. . . . The society is formal and the reverse of gay.' As for evening parties, they were 'formal beyond any possible description'. It is scarcely to be wondered at that the parties of Alba and Benavente stood out in such a sombre background.

The nobility survived the shocks of the Revolution, sinking back into conservative lethargy and political conformism. Weak though it was, there was no other class to challenge it socially until the advent of the professional politicians. There was no powerful bourgeoisie to absorb by marriage or to antagonize by privilege. The real enemy was the reforming bureaucracy and it was its heirs who swept away feudal privileges – and they were few – with the liberal legislation of the early nineteenth century. The nobility remained in its own weakness, fixed, useless and alone.

4

LOMBARDY

J. M. Roberts

ITALY, in the eighteenth century, was almost exclusively a geographical and literary term. To describe a social group as Italian at that time meant only that its members lived in the peninsula and probably spoke the Italian language. Most eighteenth-century Italians seem to have felt in this way about themselves, and thought of their society as Florentine, or Venetian, or Neapolitan first, and only in the second place, if at all, as Italian. No social group at once widespread and cohesive enough to be called Italian existed, and where there was no Italian society, there was no Italian nobility. There was only a number of societies which corresponded roughly to the political divisions of Italy, and in each of these societies there existed a separate nobility.

The distinctive marks of each of these nobilities had been evolved by the geography, social tradition and economic diversity of the various regions of Italy. In the result they differed from one another in organization, in custom and taste, in the wealth they possessed and in the power they exercised. Sardinia and the Two Sicilies were the two kingdoms of the peninsula. In each a feudal nobility was grouped about a royal court, but the resemblance between the two nobilities went no further than a superficial similarity. In language, in their relation to the king, in their military tradition, the nobles of Savoy and Piedmont were wholly dissimilar to those of Calabria and Puglia. Even within the two Sicilies there did not exist, properly speaking, one nobility; the nobility of Sicily was always distinguishable from that of the mainland. Equally striking contrasts existed between the nobles of the duchies and those of a declining Venice and the financial oligarchs of Genoa. The Papal States were a unique case; the constitutional arrangements gave a peculiar status to the Roman nobility. Among nobilities as diverse as these there is no one which can be called the *Italian* nobility of the eighteenth century.

It is not to be expected, therefore, that the Lombard nobility displays the characteristics of the other Italian nobilities. It is interesting rather for its own sake, and for its special features. It was in some ways one of the most 'European' of the Italian societies, and many of its members were closely in touch with the general movement of the Enlightenment. But in addition its social organization placed the Lombard nobility in a very special and interesting relation to the eighteenth-century phenomenon of the growth of power of the state, the phenomenon which we call Enlightened Absolutism. As an object of study the class has also the merit of being a highly developed body which is still not too large for an attempt to summarize its qualities. In the absence of a clear definition of what the status of nobility implied it is difficult to arrive at a precise enumeration of the Lombard nobles. But one estimate (that of Vianello) places the noble population of Milan at about 5000, including wives and children. At the beginning of the century Lombardy as a whole probably contained about 6500 noble persons.

In this society it was fairly easy to recognize whether a family was accepted as noble, but less easy to define what a noble family was. The nobles never formed a closed caste; they were not organized as an Estate, as elsewhere in Europe. Nobility rested on repute rather than on possession of a title, although possession of a title conferred nobility. But a title could not qualify the bearer to enter the inner circle of the Lombard families, the Patricians of Milan. Nor, strictly, was a noble title necessary for membership of this circle. These distinctions can only be explained by some reference to the origins of the Lombard nobility.

By the eighteenth century, the Lombard nobility consisted of families originally of three distinct groups, but between these groups the distinctions had become progressively more and more blurred. These groups consisted of, in the first place, the old feudal and Imperial nobility, in the second place of the Patrician families of Milan, and finally of those families which had acquired titles since the beginning of the Spanish domination of Milan. The last of these three groups was, even in the eighteenth century, of far less importance than the other two.

While the feudal nobility of the old Duchy of Milan had lost its original importance, its social pre-eminence still gave it importance in the structure of the eighteenth-century nobility. It participated in political power only in so far as its members were able to win admission to the Patrician circle, as, indeed, most of them were able to do. Originally, the feudal families had represented a political interest in the Duchy which was opposed to that of the Commune (represented by the Patricians), and they had looked to their feudal connection as a source of authority. But by the eighteenth century only their social distinction remained peculiar to them. In 1661 a member of the very old family of the Trivulzi refused the challenge of a mere *marchese* as beneath the notice of an Imperial Vassal and a Prince of the Holy Roman Empire. In the following century this might have been regarded as evidence of an exaggerated sense of status, but the social distinction deriving from a special relation to the Emperor remained the mark of the old feudal families.

In some cases these old families extended far beyond Lombardy. Their wealth, like that of all the Lombard nobles, was in land, and their estates sometimes spread all over North Italy. With the exception of the ecclesiastical corporation of the *Ospedale Maggiore* of Milan, the greatest landowners in Lombardy were the Trivulzi family. The feudal families tended to remain the richest of the Lombard nobles. Their wealth was conserved by a rigid application of the principle of primogeniture, and by that important class of instruments, the *fidecommessi*. This wealth was augmented by judicious marriage, and the Lombard nobles seem to have interpreted fairly liberally the qualifications for marriage into their class by plebeian but wealthy heiresses. But in the eighteenth century some traces of the old exclusiveness remained among the feudal families, and the marriage of a member of the great house of Stampa with the heiress of a rich merchant family still gave rise to public scandal. Marriage between the feudal and Patrician families was much more common, and even almost the general rule. In this sort of marriage, for example, the Litta family snapped up both the heiresses of the feudal lords of Albizate, a branch of the Visconti clan.

There existed no social barrier, then, between the Patricians and the old feudal families; both could draw on an equivalent antiquity of descent and both classes were equally prominent in the history of the Duchy. Together they formed its true aristocracy, and the feudal families had in addition their unique relation to the Emperor as his vassals. The feudal attributes of their tenures had dwindled by the eighteenth century to negligible proportions. Lombard feudalism was in this way unlike the Prussian and French survivals. There was no consciousness in Lombardy of the abuse of feudal privileges because these privileges did not exist to any important degree. Some estates retained as an appendage to the lordship a monopoly of milling rights, and a remnant of feudal justice was observable in the power of appointing the *Podestà* (the chief magistrate of the Commune), and in the obligation to maintain the local prisons. These relics apart, the feudal distinction of the Lombard noble was always directed upwards to the Imperial court rather than downwards towards his tenant. The tie with Vienna was never merely a formal one. A vassal owed suit at his lord's court, and there are many examples of the real consequences of this obligation.

For example, when in 1768 Gallio Trivulzio died without issue, the feudatories of Retegno and Bettola which he held of the crown fell in to Maria Theresa, his overlord, instead of reverting to another branch of the family. When in 1743 Renato Borromeo's mother wished to stop him from marrying a young lady of the Odescalchi family, he appealed to his feudal lord, again Maria Theresa, who brusquely ordered the mother not to interfere with the wishes of her vassal.

The social distinction of the Patrician families derived from their ancient status as the other element in the old nobility. They possessed a similar social eminence to that of the feudal families, but the decisively civic nature of its origins was expressed in the definition of Patrician status as the right to hold civic office in the Duchy of Milan. The formula of admission entitled the Patrician to the 'honours, prerogatives, and offices appropriate to the noble Patricians of the city of Milan'.

The pre-eminence of Milan in the political organization of Lombardy explains the pre-eminence of the Patricians as a political class. Besides their domination of the magistracies which conducted most of the administration of Lombardy (see below), the Patricians gained by the economic and commercial supremacy of the *Milanese* within Austrian Italy. In population, too, Milan was preponderant; Mantua and the counties of Lodi, Cremona and Como could never exercise an equivalent weight in affairs.

Originally the Patrician families had been drawn from the burgher and mercantile classes. Acquiring noble status relatively late in their history, they had thenceforward guarded admission to their ranks very closely. A fourteenth-century list had about two hundred families enrolled upon it, and a list of 1769 had 297. In the sixteenth century the *Congregazione degli Ordini* was formed to regulate admission, and by the end of the seventeenth century had succeeded in severing the Patrician class from its mercantile origins by recognizing all Patrician families as *ipso facto* noble, and by prescribing qualifications of positive nobility for new aspirants. From this time entrance to the class became progressively more difficult. In 1716 it was made a rule that all aspirants to Patrician status should have a majority of their possessions in the Duchy. In 1719 another decree defined the documentary proofs required of a hundred years' family residence, the specific personal nobility of the applicant and the positive nobility of his family. Later, the Austrian administration itself took a hand in this tightening-up of admission regulations; at one moment there was even talk of reverting to the exclusive list of 1377, but the notion was not pursued.

Yet it is not easy to discover how strictly these rules were observed in practice. Many of the old nobility were admitted to Patrician status, although never automatically. The Menrichi applied to enter the Patrician circle in 1651, but the application was not allowed until 1659. At the same time there were appeals from less ancient families. The Manzoni family were recognized as noble in 1771. In 1791 they applied for Patrician status, but by 1796 nothing had been done. The Pallavicino family, however, in spite of the fact that it held no land in the Duchy, was admitted to Patrician status in 1719.

It was also possible in law for a family to lose its Patrician rights, and this, too, must have rendered the boundaries of the class more fluid. Loss of status was prescribed if no member of the family had held civic office for three generations, or if a member had exercised a base trade.

The increasing homogeneity of the Lombard nobility had not therefore deprived the Patricians of their distinct legal status by the eighteenth century. Socially, by their manner of life, they were less and less distinguishable from the other nobles, and some Milanese historians regretted this, both because of the loss of the citizen character of the Patricians, and because of the lack of justification for their pretensions. But their formal distinction from the other noble families remained clear, their political privilege inviolate, as the desire of the older families to enter the Patrician class showed. Whereas any noble might be called to royal office, civic office remained reserved to the Patrician. It was for this reason that the Austrian reform of the Lombard administration in the interests of government involved the collapse of the power of the Patrician class.

After the feudal and Patrician families, the third element in the Lombard nobility was that of the large crowd of families ennobled at a comparatively recent date. This secondary, and titular, nobility was the product of the Spanish period of Milanese history. Charles V had hoped to use some of the nobility against the families of the old Ducal connection. His successors had continued a policy of creating new noble families, caressing the established ones with honours and office, and increasing the gap between the nobility and the people. The response of the new noble families was the adoption of Spanish attitudes on questions of style and prestige, and acquiescence in foreign rule.

Money seems to have been the only consistently needed qualification for entry into this nobility. It was the burden of Parini's satire on those who hoped for the purification of their plebeian blood by 'bought honours' ('*i compri onori*'). An interesting publication of the early eighteenth century, *The Nobility Unmasked*, was a more precise attack on the pretensions of many families whose riches had given them the noble standing which could hide their origins in manufacture and trade. In Litta's genealogies of the Italian families the book is attributed to Carlo della Pusterla; if this is correct, his comments are an interesting revelation of the older nobility's view of the new. The author points out that the Silva family, for example, were moneylenders in the seventeenth century, but *marchesi* in the next. The Stefani were another family which had acquired the title, and had bought up feudal estates, while at the beginning of the previous century they had merely been silk-merchants.

Nor was the rise of moneyed families the sole explanation of the new nobility's emergence; it had been Spanish policy to proliferate titles, both from a desire to win adherents and a need to reward administrative servants. And the very heavy plague casualties in seventeenth-century Lombardy were another influence; these left gaps which had to be filled by conscious policy.

Some Patrician families took up the new titles. Formerly it had been a characteristic of the Patricians that they were untitled, save for the formal appellation of *Dominus*, usually shortened to *Don*. A few Patrician families remained untitled, and the Vicar of Provision of Milan at the time of the French invasion of 1796 was a member of one of them, but the rage for titles did not leave many Patrician families unadorned. Most titles, however, were acquired by non-nobles who were rich enough to support the necessary style and fees.

A small industry existed for the manufacture of nobility. It suffered a setback in 1681 when the Spanish authorities came to consider it an abuse and garrotted the leading professional genealogist of Milan. But the market for the formally required genealogy of a noble soon revived, and a certain Bonacina made a fortune in the eighteenth century by the inventive discovery of suitable coats of arms for aspirants to quarterings. This could happen in spite of the fact that the Austrian attitude to the acquisition of new titles was less sympathetic than that of the Spanish had been. Maria Theresa had an acute sense of the dignity of nobility and attempted to check any too-easy entry to the noble class by taxation of new patents of nobility, and by regulating more strictly the purchase of feudal estates. In 1768 an Office of Heralds was set up at Milan on her initiative, and it took up the task of scrutinizing new patents and investigating old claims.

Although important distinctions of social status were observed by the Lombard nobles, most of them followed the same pattern in their social life. At its base lay a solid mass of landed wealth. The Lombard nobility was less than one per cent of the total population of the province, but it owned nearly half the total landed property. Some ennobled persons had made their money in other ways, but they all invested in land as soon as possible. The control of taxation by the local Lombard magistracies, and a general rise in agricultural prosperity kept up the luxurious standard of life always remarked by foreign travellers. This general prosperity owed much to the interest taken by the landowners themselves in the management of their estates. Smaller properties were usual in the foothills towards the north, but in the Po valley itself big estates farmed by tenant labour made some degree of experiment possible. The new large-scale plantations of rice sprang from this sort of enterprise. It required a big capital outlay to undertake the necessary irrigation, and only the greatest landlords could afford this. Nevertheless, most landlords cared for the improvement of their estates, big or small; Arthur Young noticed the huge number of agricultural pamphlets on sale at Milan. He greatly admired the farming which he saw for himself, although some of the interest displayed in it appeared too academic; at a meeting of the *Società Patriottica* he found (he says) 'a goodly company of i Marchesi, Conti, Cavalieri, Abati, but not one close-cropped wig, or a dirty pair of breeches to give authority to their proceedings'.

At the same time this mass of landed wealth was irrigated by profits made in financial and commercial transactions. Sometimes this came to the nobility indirectly by marriage; sometimes it came directly, by nobles taking part in business. The Greppi family made their fortunes by tax-farming in Lombardy and by trading at Cadiz. The *marchese* Molo held the bulk of the capital in a company lending money to the Austrian government during the Seven Years War.

This great wealth was preserved in a stable form by the institutions of primogeniture and *fidecommessi* – which also severely restricted the amount of land available for purchase by would-be noble families. It was an implication of these institutions that younger sons could not expect to inherit any important portion of the family capital. This being so, it was likely that only the eldest son would have the means sufficient to support the family town house and its accustomed routine, and to enter upon the career of municipal office which was the usual activity of the head of the family. Gorani, in his memoirs, commented that the French Revolution was made by discontented younger sons, and he was thinking of discontented sons who applauded the French invasion of Lombardy. Where there was no provision for them from the family fortune the younger sons were bound to the more fortunate eldest brother upon whose charity they had to rely. The family of Verri, the economist, was split for years by a quarrel about a disputed inheritance.

This made such careers as were available to the nobility of great importance, since they drew off the energy and talent which might otherwise have rendered Lombard society unstable. Education other than a professional training could fit the sons of the nobility only for the drawing-room. The two colleges of the liberal professions of law and medicine did better, and the college of the *Nobili Giureconsulti* was the usual prelude to a civic career, though not to private practice, which was rarely taken up by nobles. In medicine, the father of Melzi d'Eril (the vice-president of Bonaparte's Italian Republic) was a general practitioner at Magenta. But Melzi was a poor man, and few nobles with a medical training had ever to make their living by means of it. Rather more typical is the figure of Carlo Archinto, who became director of the *Ospedale Maggiore*. (He had also the distinction of having been made a grandee of Spain by both sides in the War of the Spanish Succession.)

A more important receptacle for younger sons than either of the professions was the Austrian service. There had previously existed the possibility of service with the Spanish, and the Rusconi family continued in the eighteenth century to provide officers for the Spanish army, while members of the Castiglioni served in both Austrian and Spanish forces. But it was usual for Lombards to serve the Emperor alone. Within the province itself opportunities were limited. The command of the castle of Milan was an important one, and in 1728 went to an Italian for the first time since Charles V. A kinsman of this officer, a Visconti, served in the Imperial army against the Turks, and rose to become a magnate of Hungary. He is said to have been of the greatest ability, and only the fact that he could not write held him back from even higher preferment.

Sometimes advancement could carry an able man very far indeed. A Serbelloni was a field-marshal, and Charles VI appointed a Borromeo and a Visconti at different times as viceroys at Naples. The *marchese* Botta who was ambassador at St. Petersburg may have been a Lombard. But the most spectacular of these Lombard careers was that of Count Ludovico Barbiano Belgioiso. He served in the Seven Years War at first as a captain of grenadiers, and later as a brigadier. In 1764 he was appointed Ambassador to Sweden. In 1769 he changed this embassy for that at London, where he remained until 1783. During visits to the Continent he became the confidential friend of the young Joseph II, who made him Minister Plenipotentiary and vice-Governor in the Netherlands in 1783. He was present at Joseph's death-bed as a trusted friend.

One other service entered by young Lombards deserves a word of mention. This was the Order of the Knights of St. John, the Knights of Malta. Young nobles could enter the Order for a few years, during which they learned something about seamanship, saw, possibly, some fighting against pirates, and carried out the never very onerous garrison duties of Valetta. But the Order was decayed, and the service given to it can hardly be classed with that given to the Imperial forces.

The other career to which younger sons were destined, and in numbers probably the most important, was the Church. It was even more important for daughters. In early eighteenth-century Italy marriage and the convent were the only alternatives presented to the Italian girl of gentle birth. It is only towards the end of the century that one begins to find in the pages of Litta the names of unmarried daughters who did not enter convents. But it is not easy to see exactly what convent life meant. Some houses appear to have taken only noble novices, admitting no plebeian, and this makes one suspect that appropriate relaxations of discipline were not unknown. *Santa Barbara* was a house of this sort. In some others, families reserved the same rooms from one generation to the next, and the occupants enjoyed considerable comfort. One reason for the outcry against the closing of religious houses by Joseph II may have been the handicap which he thus imposed on parents who had to dispose of unemployable or unmarriageable children.

So large was the number of Lombard nobles entering the Church that it was inevitable that the Lombard families should be well represented in the higher ranks of the clergy. Out of ten sons of the Archinto family, seven were in orders of one kind or another during the century. One of them was an Archbishop of Milan and two were cardinals, one being a Papal Secretary of State and the other a *Nuncio*. The Castiglioni produced twenty-one clergy, but this total included some canons of Castiglione, where the family had special responsibilities. The others numbered amongst themselves an Archbishop and a Jesuit missionary to Tonkin. The largest of the Lombard clans, the Visconti, raised twenty-nine clergy during the century, and thirty-three nuns. The priests included an Archbishop of Milan, a *Nuncio* and a General of Jesuits. Finally, Clement XIII was himself a Rezzonico from Como.

These professional, military and ecclesiastical connections were the outworks of the Lombard nobility's main strength, which was to be found, of course, in the political power of those who had succeeded to the family patrimony. But although the latter is the central topic in any comment on the Lombard nobility, this remarkable and widespread connection sometimes disposed of real influence and power, and can properly be regarded as European in extent. The centre of Lombard life, however, was Milan, and it was only in the capital that the nobles lived in close association with one another. Most of the old great families kept up country houses, but it was the *palazzi* of Milan which set the style of their social life.

It was a life of the greatest luxury. In 1766 Alessandro Verri went to Versailles; he thought it compared poorly with the splendour of the *Palazzo Litta*. Foreign visitors throughout the century commented on the luxury of Milan. Maria Theresa was constantly worried about the *'pompa esterna'* of her Milanese subjects, and in 1769 promulgated a series of sumptuary laws to restrain them. She may have been afraid that the archducal court would suffer an eclipse. Both because of the prestige of those who displayed it, and because of the employment which it generated, the luxury of the noble houses was a social fact of the greatest significance. To live *more nobilium* was itself a mark of caste, and was accepted by the Office of Heralds as one evidence of nobility. It might express itself in the maintenance of a private theatre – such as that of the Pertusati – or in the decoration of a church to the greater glory of the decorators – as the Trivulzi did at *San Stefano*, and the Borromeo family at the *Grazie* – but it was always an important social fact. In some cases the profusion was bound to spill over into vulgarity. A comment of Lalande has been quoted: 'The character of the Milanese nobles is marked by generosity and munificence; they entertain in the most friendly manner in both town and country; in the Italian cities a foreigner is sure of a good reception, and their tables make even the French look small. However, a great many of them have not yet acquired *bon ton*.'

The cultural function of this profusion is more easily appreciated. Just as political life was confined to the nobility, so was cultural life; the non-nobles who enjoyed it or contributed to it did so as hangers-on. The nobility which Parini satirized was his only audience, and without its patronage he could hardly have written at all.

Pietro Verri said once *'Noi viviamo in umbra mortis'*. He had an interest in painting the picture as darkly as possible in order to make the contrast with his own enlightened circle a sharp one. Also, he spoke from the point of view of a culture much more European and Encyclopaedist than that of most of his class; he was inevitably disparaging in his judgements on more traditional cultural approaches. He did not give a fair picture of the state of Milan before he wrote. It is true that at the beginning of the century Lombard culture was a narrowly provincial thing, but this provinciality was quickly assailed by French influences. The first impulse seems to have come from the invasions of the War of the Spanish Succession and the arrival of the French commander Vaudemont. It was Vaudemont who began at Milan the practice of inviting ladies and gentlemen to be present at the same *conversazioni*, and who thus introduced into Milan that powerful engine of Enlightenment, the *salon*. When the thought of the Enlightenment came to Milan it came directly through French channels, and by mid-century the *salons* of the Duchess Serbelloni and the Countess Borromeo were known for gallophile sympathies which were political as well as cultural.

The predominant literary flavour of contemporary Italian culture gave rise to the *accademie*, circles where literary and philosophical discussion took place under the patronage and at the hospitality of some great noble. The *Trasformati* were the most famous of these groups, and were the centre of the Imbonati-Borromeo society. The defects of this culture, and its determination to take itself more seriously than its achievements would warrant, stand out clearly enough. But it was a culture from which sprang the Palatine Society and the publication of Muratori's *Rerum Italicum Scriptores*, one of the great monuments of Italian historical scholarship. It was at the same time that the Trivulzio collection of manuscripts was formed, the basis of the later *Trivulziana* library. The private library of the *marchese* Pertusati went in a similar way to form the nucleus of Brera. The self-assurance of the economists and reformers of the Lombard Enlightenment has distracted attention from this less glamorous but firm literary culture, the product of the noble society of Milan in the first half of the eighteenth century. It was one of the most impressive achievements of the Lombard nobility.

Austria and the Lombard nobles

The relations of the Lombard nobility with the Imperial government are the core of the story of the class during the century. There were two parts to the story, the relation of the class to the growth of state power in the second half of the century, and the establishment of Austrian rule in the first place. The latter is the story of the gradual settling down of relations between individual families and the Austrian administration, and of the gradual realization that the Austrians had come to stay; it does not require a lengthy description.

On 19th December 1700, Philip V was proclaimed in Milan. Shortly afterwards a French army occupied the Duchy. From this time until the end of the Franco-Spanish occupation of 1743–6 the Senate, the expression of the corporate personality of the Lombard nobility, easily adapted its allegiance to each new *de facto* sovereign. It always allied itself with the occupying power. The gradual settling down of family loyalties on the side of Austria and the slow evaporation of Spanish connections with the passage of time went on quietly, but did not restrain the opportunism of the Senate. When the Austrians finally returned in 1746 they launched the only political persecution which Milan was to see until the revolutionary invasion of 1796. The Countess Borromeo fled to Bergamo, a Rezzonico to Rome and a Melzi to Brescia. One noble was pursued on Venetian territory, taken, tried and executed. He was the only one, and within a few years the exiles had returned. This was the end of opposition to Austrian rule. The significant feature of the whole period is that no Lombard ever suggested that Lombardy should be independent. All that was ever in question was the identity of the occupying power, not its rights. This throws an interesting light on the supineness of the Lombard nobles in the crisis of the destruction of their power later in the century. They could only irritate a government, and never resist it.

It is the second half of the century which is the period of the struggle over reforms, or rather over the rationalization of government: it is this period which is the most interesting episode in the story of the Lombard nobility. The key to the struggle is the fact that the whole constitution of Lombardy was jeopardized by any attempt at reform, and this meant in turn that the political supremacy of the Lombard nobility was bound to be called in question, because constitutional privilege in Lombardy was confined to that class. What was implied can be seen from a summary of the constitutional arrangements of Lombardy as they existed through most of the first half of the century. There were three main agencies of government. Ultimate authority was vested in the Council of Italy (formerly the Council of Spain) at Vienna. The government at Milan had the responsibility for promulgating the decrees of Vienna, and for supervising their execution; it consisted for effective purposes of the Governor, helped by a *Gran Cancelliere*, who presided over the *Consiglio Segreto*, a consultative council. The third agency involved was the local Lombard administrative system itself, and in its charge rested the day-to-day administration of the province. In the organs which made up this system lay the main strength of the Lombard nobles.

But it would be more exact not to speak of a 'system' in connection with Lombard administration, for the organs that ran the administration were independent, unarticulated and usually autonomous within their own spheres. It was neither a royal nor a centralized administration; the powers of the various bodies derived from no central source, and there was no vital organ standing above the rest in a hierarchy of administration, for no hierarchy existed. It consisted of a series of independent magistracies, operating largely through judicial forms, and each of them enjoyed a more or less complete independence of the rest.

The nobility had an effective monopoly of places in these magistracies, and, because of the predominance of Milan within the province, the Milanese Patricians tended to usurp a predominant rôle within the nobility. The government of Milan itself was in the hands of the Patricians alone, and was one of the most important of the independent magistracies. This was the *Consiglio di Commune* of Milan, the sixty Decurions, who appointed a Vicar of Provision and twelve magistrates to exercise the functions of city government between meetings of the general council. These magistrates, in turn, appointed justices to specific duties. The Decurions were what would now be called an 'omnibus' authority, exercising all sorts of governmental functions within a given area. An example of another kind of magistracy, exercising important powers in a narrower field, was the *Senato*, the senior magistracy, with wide judicial attributes. But the Senate, too, had some administrative functions. Similarly quasi-judicial and quasi-administrative were the *Magistrato Ordinario* and the *Magistrato Straordinario*. These divided between them the financial administration of central and local government, and each maintained its own police and legal apparatus. The *Congregazione di Stato* was not strictly a magistracy, but was appointed by representatives from the whole of Lombardy to advise upon governmental policy from a local point of view, and to give rulings on minor questions of administration. There existed no mediator between these bodies if they came into conflict unless the dispute fell within the jurisdiction of the Senate.

In the absence of a royal administration a Governor had necessarily to abandon much of his authority to the magistracies because of his dependence upon them. Until the supremacy of the state was unequivocally asserted during the reigns of Maria Theresa and Joseph, the power of the magistracies, the network of local right and privilege, and the pretensions of the city of Milan make it difficult to find an Austinian sovereign. The legal sovereignty of the Austrian crown meant little in the face of the real powers of the Lombard nobility. Pietro Verri remarked that there had been set up 'an opaque and resistant body between sovereign and people'. It was the aim of the Enlightened Absolutist to remove this barrier, and to leave the subject face to face with the state.

In the struggle against the Austrian reforms the nobility raised a cry with a deceptively modern ring, the claim that they were defending the rights and independence of Lombardy against government by foreigners (as opposed to formal subjection to *a* foreign government, to which they did not object). The personalities of the Austrian governors and their Italian, but non-Lombard, assistants did much to enrage the nobility, who regarded local administration as their own preserve. The noble claim to defend local interests was valid in the sense that the nobles alone were political Lombardy, and that no other class had a hearing, but it seems less valid if the interests of the rest of the population are considered. As late as 1772 the Senate was still voting for the retention of torture in the penal system. The nobles had a class-interest in opposing reform, and few of them recognized the partiality of their views. In the nature of the case they were bound to adopt a sterile and negative attitude, for they had nothing to gain from the rationalization of government, and everything to lose. Their interest was to keep things as they were, and their strongest weapon was the inertia of any collegiate body. Reforms could be resisted for years in a maze of discussion by the privileged bodies which had to be consulted.

This meant that the problem facing the Austrian government was as much one of creating a new centralized administration as of destroying the obstructive power of the magistracies. But because the stimulus to reform was in the first place a need for more revenue, the problem was seen by the advisers of Charles VI as financial rather than administrative. In the beginning they still hoped that they could rely on the carrying out of new financial regulations by the local magistracies. This was the course attempted by the *Giunta* set up by Miro, but almost at once this body met its match in the stone-walling tactics of the nobles. Its attempts to increase the fiscal obligations of property were swamped by a flood of appeals to the Senate. Moreover, even the slight hope of success on the part of the *Giunta* was destroyed by the Franco-

Spanish occupation of 1743; its failure to make headway before this, however, had shown where the crux of the Lombard problem lay, that is to say, in the struggle with privilege within the administration. Under Maria Theresa, financial necessity again caused the problem to be approached first as one of revenue. The struggle with Prussia and the example of that relatively poor state were important factors in the reforms of the state mechanism in Austria and Bohemia, and the same was true of Lombardy. There was even a plan for the creation of a Lombard army of 30,000 men to be supported from local resources. Under Maria Theresa, therefore, the story of the Lombard nobility becomes inseparable from the story of the Austrian machinery of state.

The essential step in overcoming the handicaps imposed on government in Lombardy was the creation of a skeleton administration which for the first time by-passed the magistracies and was insulated from noble influence. A beginning was made in 1749 by the creation of a royal fiscal organ, the *Tribunale del Censo*, dominated by the great Tuscan reformer, Pompeo Neri. He instituted a new *censimento* embodying the previously ineffective reforms; it was as detested as its predecessor, but much more effective. Its effectiveness sprang from the organization under the *Tribunale* of a new fiscal bureaucracy. It was an independent hierarchy, and in each commune there acted as its agent a royal official, the *Cancelliero*, and in each province a royal delegate. At the same time local councils hitherto responsible for the sharing of tax burdens inside the commune were enlarged to include all landowners, and not merely the nobility.

The significance of these steps was very large. Their aim had been financial, but they affected the position of the old administrative oligarchy in a vital point, that of its previous indispensability to the government. The new pattern of an independent administration was now workable. Orders could for the first time go down the chain of command without dilution. Also, and very significantly, the government was for the first time brought into direct contact with local life, and even with the individual subject, instead of the resilient corporate bodies. Even the inclusion of all landowners in the local councils was significant for the tactical opportunity it gave to the government of calling upon allies against the Patrician hegemony within these bodies. But much remained to be done. Appeals for reduced tax assessments could still be heard and allowed by the Patrician *Magistrato Camerale*, and were still thwarting the intentions of the Vienna government. Firmian reported in 1760 that a still more radical cure was necessary if ever Milan was to recover its economic and administrative well-being. In fact, an entire reconstruction of the administration had already begun, and took over thirty years to complete.

The beginnings of the destruction of Patrician power can be traced back to the appointment in 1753 of the Minister Plenipotentiary to assist the Governor. He was much more the direct instrument of Vienna than the Governor had been. The new position of Italian affairs in the Austrian state was defined by the abolition of the Council of Italy in 1757, and the transference of Italian affairs to a simple department of the Imperial Chancery. In this body, unlike the old Council, there were no representatives of the Lombard Senate.

Inside Lombardy the high period of reform began with the creation of a supreme Economic Council in 1765. As a final court of appeal in financial matters it also centralized in itself all existing financial authority. It also took in hand the business of judicial reform, and in 1767 the Senate lost its jurisdiction of ecclesiastical questions, and in 1771 all its non-judicial functions. As the senior magistracy, the reduction of the Senate was fundamental to the process of reform.

But the climax of the rationalization of government only came with Joseph II, who was willing to carry the process far beyond the limits envisaged by the advisers of Maria Theresa. In 1786 the Senate, the *Magistrato Camerale*, the *Congregazione di Stato* and all the remaining judicial immunities were abolished. A new *Consiglio di Governo*, working through six departments, replaced them. All the local administrative boundaries were changed, and the City of Milan was made responsible to the *Intendenza Politica*, the end of Milanese supremacy in local affairs being brought about by the simple absorption of the city in the general structure of local government as one department among the rest.

These changes were the end of the formal predominance of the Patricians, and an indication of how enfeebled their resistance had been. One of the reasons for this feebleness was the existence within the nobility of a group of young nobles who approved of the change, at least before it came about. They hoped for a reform of government in the interests of public prosperity, which they conceived in larger terms than had their fathers. Gabriele Verri, one of the last representatives of the older generation, died in 1782; his sons, Alessandro and Pietro, were prominent in the generation that had come to maturity around 1760. Their circle of young reformers included the young Melzi, Beccaria, Gorani, the Duchess Serbelloni and the Countess Imbonati. They drew largely on French and British political and economic ideas, more especially the latter, and between 1760 and 1780 conducted something in the nature of a propaganda campaign for reform. Some of them took an active part in the reorganization of government, and the name of Verri is usually linked with the reform of the Farm of Taxes, but the group was led logically along the same path as the Austrian government, from financial reform to the destruction of privilege. But while Joseph II was animated by something of the spirit of Hobbes, Verri's motives were rather those of an Adam Smith.

Verri led the attack on the Constitutions of Charles V, for example, by arguing that they impeded commerce by diverting cases to autonomous judicial bodies, and bogging them down in litigation. His motive was the improvement of public prosperity by the removal of hindrances to the free circulation of trade, and he was led from this to attack privileged corporations. An emphasis on economic affairs is characteristic of the reformers among the Lombard nobility. Only Beccaria, the penologist, had anything important to say on other questions. This makes their writing seem tedious today. It also emphazises the lack of interest of their political ideas except in so far as they were committed to increasing the power of the state as an engine of reform.

The state had to undertake the burden of the attack on the 'despotismo togato' of the Patricians. This is the essential theme of the political ideas of the reforming nobles. But as they were themselves nobles, they did not envisage the revolution in the status of their class which was to follow the destruction of their political power. Nor did they see the political problem as one of placing restraints on power regardless of its location, for they saw it as exclusively one of sovereignty. Pietro Verri stated the reformers' view of the problem: 'Public happiness and true well-being make me desire that the government of men shall cease and that of laws shall begin, and that the sacred right of making law shall be jealously reserved to the crown alone'. The question of sovereignty could hardly be stated more plainly.

But the reformers themselves began to lose faith in the state towards the end of Joseph's reign. With the abolition of privilege went increasingly obvious restraint of personal freedom. Pietro Verri's letters to his brother were often opened, and obstructive old Patricians were roughly handled by a state police which was no longer hampered by a fear of infringing privilege. The reformers began to regret the humiliation of their class. Above all, it was useless for Lombards any longer to hope to influence the policy of Vienna. Once there had been some reciprocal confidence between Austrian and Lombard members of the administration, but it was no longer possible to retain any independence while working for Joseph. The reformers became as suspect at Vienna as were the opponents of reform. They themselves turned their thoughts to the device of a written constitution as a defence against the encroachments of royal power.

It was at this juncture that Joseph II died. During his reign the political power of the Lombard nobles had come to an end, and the reign of his successor, Leopold, only emphasized this. On 6th May 1790, the Lombard people were ordered to state their grievances and wishes, and for a moment it seemed that there was a possibility that the Patricians might step back into their old place. But in the event there were concessions to local feeling, but no cession of royal authority, which remained as absolute as before. A new *Congregazione di Stato* was set up, but it could only offer advice when consulted by the government. The forms of the machinery of central administration were reshaped, but no representative element was admitted. On the principle of the sovereignty of the state there was no compromise, for neither the Senate nor the magistracies, the old bulwarks of noble power, were restored.

Milan on the eve of the invasion of 1796 showed signs that the social status of the nobles was beginning to be questioned as their political privilege had been. Revolutionary elements were entering the city from the south, and some Lombards were looking forward to a French invasion. The nobility were divided amongst themselves against this new threat, and Verri, Melzi, Francesco Visconti and their friends acquired the name and reputation of 'jacobins', and the suspicion of their families. One noble was even a member of the Jacobin Club at Paris.

The old dominance of the nobles had derived from their being coterminous with the social, political and cultural élite of their society. By 1796 this substantial unity had gone, as had their political power, and with these things had gone the special character of the old Lombard nobility. After the departure of the Austrians in May 1796 the local radicals began almost at once to attack the Decurions and the Patricians, and among their leaders were a Serbelloni, a Visconti, and a Trivulzio. The eventual absorption of the nobles into the service of the Napoleonic Empire by Napoleon and Melzi d'Eril only registered the loss of their special character which had already taken place.

5
PRUSSIA
A. Goodwin

BETWEEN the accession of Frederick the Great and the outbreak
of the French Revolution the nobility in Prussia enjoyed a
brief heyday of real power, effective leadership and relative
prosperity. Before 1740 the political predominance and provincial independence of this aristocracy had been endangered
by the growth of Prussian absolutism. After the death of
Frederick, its prestige as a class withered under the social
criticism of the *Aufklärung*, and its economic resources were
sapped by an out-moded system of feudal land-tenure. The
play of economic forces and its own conservatism would,
indeed, most likely have ruined the Prussian nobility at that
stage, had it not been saved by the reforms of Stein and
Hardenberg. The history of the nobility in eighteenth-century
Prussia is thus largely the story of its preservation, first by an
Enlightened Despot and then by the liberal reformers. Frederick
the Great prevented seventeenth-century absolutism and middle-
class rivalry from curtailing further the political powers and
administrative significance of the nobility. The liberal reformers ensured its survival in the changed conditions of the
nineteenth century by disrupting the social system of Frederick II and by allowing free scope to the doctrines of Adam
Smith. In this essay an attempt will be made to explain why,
in Prussia, Enlightened Despotism was the ally and not the
enemy of the nobility and why, after 1789, economic liberalism
did not sacrifice the aristocracy to the middle-class.

In the second half of the seventeenth century Frederick

William, the Great Elector, had found that the creation of a standing army and a civil service had involved him in serious conflicts with his feudal nobility. Despite this he had abridged their provincial liberties and attenuated their corporate independence. In the Rhenish-Westphalian districts of Cleve-Mark the local estates, dominated by the nobility, had been deprived of their right to negotiate independently with foreign powers, and had abandoned their former practice of bringing before the Emperor complaints against the infraction of their constitutional prerogatives. They had been compelled to accept Prussian garrisons and to contribute regularly to the cost of a standing army. They had, however, maintained their *Indigenatsrecht*, which prescribed that all public officials should be recruited exclusively from natives of the province and hold landed property therein. The provincial assembly continued to hold annual sessions, irrespective of a summons by the Elector, and, in general, the nobility still remained particularist in feeling and inclined to look for guidance and support either to the Dutch or the Emperor. In East Prussia the political leaders, who had attempted to withhold the recognition of Hohenzollern sovereignty in concert with the Polish nobility, had either been imprisoned for life or executed. The provincial assembly had been restricted to the consideration of fiscal business and Frederick William had succeeded in sowing dissension between the nobility and the two other estates. In the Electoral Mark the conflict with the estates was less embittered, but ended more decisively in favour of the dynasty. After a four-year struggle, in which the *Landtag* (provincial Diet) had been repeatedly dissolved, the estates had consented, in 1653, to vote a fixed annual sum for six years as their contribution to the upkeep of the standing army. In return, Frederick William had confirmed all their existing prerogatives and maintained the social and fiscal privileges of the nobility. This settlement, regarded by the estates as the palladium of their liberties, in fact marked the end of the political powers of the provincial assembly. In the eighteenth century the general or plenary

Landtag of the Electoral Mark was only summoned to pay homage to new sovereigns on their accession. Committees of the estates, it is true, met from time to time and a credit institution, under their control – the *Kurmärkische Landschaft* – survived till 1820, but that was all. The effective activity of the estates was henceforth confined to the more restricted area of the *Kreise* or circles, which were in law seignorial corporations enjoying a measure of self-government. At the beginning of the eighteenth century public affairs within the circle were discussed in a representative assembly or diet, and relations with the central authority were maintained through a rural councillor, or *Landrat*, who was almost invariably a noble and was chosen by the estates as their representative rather than the king's. In other words, centralization had stopped short at the smallest unit of public administration in the country districts, though the economy of the towns had been subjected to the control of bureaucratic taxation officials, known as *Steuerräte*.

The Prussian nobility, despite their loss of political independence, had thus been left with their social and fiscal privileges intact, their rights of patrimonial jurisdiction over their feudal tenants undisturbed and a secure hold on the day-to-day administration of the country districts. Absolutism had not gone far enough to provoke the same kind of aristocratic reaction in Prussia as occurred in eighteenth-century France. This became evident during the reign of Frederick William I. Under this king the dynasty still maintained steady pressure on the nobility, but the estates had, by then, grown accustomed to registering merely formal protests and, for the most part, the nobles offered only passive resistance to such legislative innovations as threatened their interests.

The clearest evidence of such discrimination against the nobility is to be found in Frederick William's economic and fiscal policy. One of the first acts of the king after his accession had been to convert the whole complex of territories, domains and estates of the house of Hohenzollern into a perpetual

Fideikommiss, or family landed trust. The main practical effect was to establish the legal principle of the indivisibility of all the royal possessions. This family law of 13th August 1713 also forbade the encumbrance or alienation of the crown domain lands, and thus brought into discredit the previous practice of farming out the domain by means of leases of inheritance. This was the beginning of a revolution in the management of the royal estates, which, it should be noted, formed no less than one-third of the total arable area of Prussia. Short-term leases, valid only for six years, now became customary and leaseholding on the domain was confined to the middle-classes. This important discrimination against the nobility led to the rise of an increasingly powerful group of bourgeois estate-managers, who, as representatives of the royal authority, exercised jurisdictional and other functions in these districts. The resumption of crown lands became more frequent and Frederick William did not scruple to buy up encumbered noble estates in order to round off his possessions. In Poland and the Swedish Baltic provinces large areas of the royal domains had passed into the hands of the nobility. Frederick William's sharp reversal of previous domain policy prevented a similar tendency making itself felt in Prussia.

The king also resumed the attack on the fiscal privileges of the nobility. He began in East Prussia, where the nobility, ever since the days of the Teutonic Order, had never enjoyed complete immunity from taxation. Seizing on this as a pretext, Frederick William carried out between 1716 and 1720 a much-needed consolidation of various direct taxes in the form of a general hide tax or *Generalhufenstoss.* Previously the main incidence of the hide, poll and cattle taxes in this area had been on the peasantry, for their assessment had been in the hands of aristocratic officials. Tax evasion by the nobility was now arrested and a more uniform and equitable system of land taxation was thereby achieved. It was in this context that Frederick William made his much-quoted boast that he was 'ruining the authority of the Junkers and establishing Prussian sovereignty like a rock of bronze'. The attempt, however, to reform the land-tax systems of the other parts of his dominions, where the nobility could appeal to its traditional fiscal immunities, was a dismal failure. For this set-back Frederick William sought compensation, in 1717, by introducing, in the central provinces of the Electoral Mark and Magdeburg, a scheme for the commutation of feudal knight-service. Ever since the establishment of the standing army this form of personal service had been obsolete, and the last time it had been performed had been in 1701. The new money payment or *Lehnpferdegeld* was therefore regarded by the king's tenants-in-chief as an unjustifiable exaction, especially as they had not been consulted in advance. Nor could they forget that their liability to knight-service, nominal though it had become, afforded the technical justification for their freedom from taxation. The inducement to make the change was simply the king's declared willingness to transform these feudal tenures into allodial property and thus to give his vassals full power of disposal over their landed possessions. The power to mortgage or sell such property inevitably seemed a doubtful and suspect advantage to the nobility, whose main source of income was still the land. This measure so provoked the nobles of the Old Mark and Magdeburg that they even appealed against it to the Imperial Aulic Council and only paid the levy at the sword's point. The king, however, never wavered in his determination to implement his policy and to extend it to other provinces.

Under Frederick William the process of centralization culminated in the fusion of the dual system of public finance, the formation, in the provinces, of the War and Domain Chambers, and, at the centre, of the General Directory. One result of this expansion of the civil service was that the administrative as well as the political powers of the provincial estates were now threatened. In disaffected areas, such as the Old Mark and Magdeburg, the king even refused to allow the diets of the circles to present candidates of their own for the office of *Landrat* and nominated these agents himself. A firmer dis-

cipline over the royal vassals was also enforced and the economic situation, activities and general behaviour of the nobility
were minutely recorded in the lists and registers known as
Vassallentabelle, kept by the War and Domain Chambers. The
nobles were strictly forbidden to enter the service of foreign
armies or states; they were not allowed, except with the king's
permission, to travel abroad, and then only for short periods
and for urgent personal reasons. Their sons had the greatest
difficulty in obtaining leave to make the 'grand tours', which
European nobilities in the eighteenth century had come to
regard as an indispensable part of their general education. An
embargo was also enforced against young Prussian nobles
attending foreign universities. One of the main purposes of
this officious and prying despotism was to force the nobility,
even against its will, to adopt the military profession and to
enter the corps of officers.

The suspicion with which Frederick William regarded his
nobility strongly coloured his political testament of 1722. In
general, the king advised his heir that he might find it expedient
to show grace and indulgence to the nobles as a social class,
but was careful to recommend that he should distinguish the
good from the bad. He suggested that, by meting out the
appropriate rewards and punishments, Frederick might even
inspire devotion as well as fear. It was evident, however, that
the king regarded the nobles as the most troublesome of his
subjects. Frederick William singled out as the most dangerous
to the dynasty the great nobles of East Prussia. He adjured his
son to keep a watchful eye on the Finck and Dohna families,
otherwise he would find that they would become co-rulers
with him in this province. He also used harsh words of the
nobles of the Cleves-Mark area, whom he described as 'dumb
oxen, but as malicious as the devil'. He had recently suspended
the annual sessions of their provincial assembly and had only
restored them after the estates had promised to be less im-
petuous and recalcitrant in future. The nobility of the lower
Rhine were contemptuously dismissed as bad managers, living

beyond their means, and still Dutch or Imperialist in sympathy and outlook. Frederick William explicitly warned his son against employing in the public service his stupid and self-willed vassals in the Westphalian districts of Minden and Ravensberg. From the Schulenburgs, Alvensleben's and Bismarcks in the Old Mark and Magdeburg his successor could only expect stiff-necked independence and cantankerous opposition. Even when compelled to recognize the loyalty of his vassals in the New Mark, just east of the Oder, the king felt it necessary to qualify his appreciation by emphasizing their ingrained habit of grumbling. The only provincial nobility with whom he could find no fault were the inhabitants of Pomerania. These estimates, in so far as they were not just the result of the king's splenetic temperament, show that the political problem of reconciling the Prussian nobility to the absolutist and militarist state was still unsolved. Nor was the situation substantially different as Frederick William's reign drew to its close.

The accession of Frederick the Great marked a new and important stage in the relations between the Hohenzollern dynasty and the Prussian nobility. The period of antagonism and conflict, which had lasted for a century, now ended and gave place to one of co-operation and understanding. The most pressing need for the dynasty to offer the aristocracy a 'New Deal' arose from Frederick the Great's determination to conquer Silesia. The series of wars which resulted rendered internal political conflicts unthinkable. By 1740, moreover, Hohenzollern sovereignty in the outlying provinces had been accepted and vindicated. Absolutism had won the protracted duel with the estates, and Prussia was now free to concentrate on the conquest of great-power status in Europe. The personality of the new king also facilitated a change of attitude toward the nobility. Whereas Frederick William I had been bourgeois in his tastes and sympathies, Frederick II had the habits, culture and social prejudices of the aristocracy. It was not long before the king described the Prussian nobility not only as 'the fairest jewels of his crown', but as 'the foundations and pillars of the state'. The trust which the sovereign reposed in his new allies was amply justified by events. At the end of the second Silesian war in 1748, Frederick could say to the nobility: 'Your sons are the defenders of their country and their stock is so good that it deserves to be preserved at all costs'. A few years later, in his political testament of 1752, the king declared that the preservation of the nobility was one of the main political objectives of the monarchy. Other aristocracies might be richer, but none, he thought, was so brave or so loyal. The contrast between this document and the political testament of 1722 is striking. Frederick was no more blind to the personal deficiencies of some of the Prussian nobles than his father, and his contempt for a mere court nobility was even more pronounced. But whereas Frederick William could not help minimizing, his son did his best to exalt and magnify the qualities and achievements of the Prussian nobles. In 1722 the sovereign could find only one section of the nobility which he could bring himself to praise; in 1752 the ruler could find only one section – that of Cleves – which he could unreservedly condemn. Frederick's comments on the idiosyncracies of the noble inhabitants of the various provinces are, however, just as revealing as those of his father. The East Prussians he regarded as skilful and active, but inclined to be rooted in their local concerns. The Pomeranians, solid and dependable stateservants, were lacking in the finesse required in diplomacy. The nobles of the Mark Brandenburg were, he thought, too much subject to the distracting influence of the capital, but, nevertheless, devoted and loyal. Those who stood highest in the king's estimation were the inhabitants of Magdeburg, who had provided Frederick with some of his most eminent collaborators. The Westphalians from Mark and Minden were an excellent stock, lacking perhaps in *savoir-faire* and deficient in the social graces, but reliable and hard-working. Frederick, however, described the nobles of Cleves as imbecile, confused and degenerate, and these strictures were not unwarranted, for by the end of the century, the nobles of this province had become practically extinct. It is true also that the king had to make allowances for the stupidity and Austrian outlook of the Silesian nobility, and even in 1768, when Frederick wrote his second political testament, this section of the community had not been fully assimilated.

The quality which the Prussian autocrat most appreciated in his subjects was devoted service to the state. This loyalty was most valuable in the army and Frederick made it his immediate aim to overcome the previous reluctance of the nobility to enter the corps of officers. Here persuasion and preference were soon found to yield better dividends than compulsion. The king made it clear, however, from the outset that he expected his nobles, provided they were able-bodied, to serve in the army and found ways and means of bringing home his displeasure to those who discouraged their sons from adopting a military career. Before 1740 it had usually been hard economic necessity which had driven the sons of the Prussian nobility to adopt such a poorly-paid profession. Frederick, however, was reluctant to allow the officer corps to be used as a means of providing even temporary outdoor relief for the impecunious youth of the aristocracy. He taught the nobles to regard the army as a permanent career and did his best to discourage officers from resigning their commissions on succeeding to family estates. To endow the officer class with *esprit de corps* he turned it into the preserve of the nobility. It was indeed not so much the nobility as the corps of officers which became a caste in eighteenth-century Prussia. During the Seven Years War, Frederick failed to maintain this monopoly, because the supply of officers of noble extraction was not sufficient to meet the army's urgent needs. As soon as the war was over, however, middle-class officers were retired or transferred to artillery regiments or garrison duties. This cult of the superior military virtues, with which the king credited the nobility, was sometimes carried to excess. It was, for example, one of Frederick's foibles, when reviewing his troops, to believe that officers whose names he could not recall were not noble. If he adhered to this view, as he sometimes did, the unlucky officer stood in serious danger of losing his commission. Though it was his settled principle to recruit his armies, so far as possible, from the inhabitants of Prussia, the king preferred to appoint foreign nobles to the officer corps rather than fall back on the middle-class. The reality behind this prejudice was that the middle-class had been exempted from military service, and thus had little chance of acquiring the habit of command or the sentiment of honour characteristic of the nobility. The middle-class might swell the treasury receipts through the excise, but it was only the nobility which could provide the army with its moral backbone. The Frederician rule of promotion by seniority was one which accorded well with the interests and conceptions of the nobility and the open favour and precedence now accorded to the officer class offered a bait which was difficult to resist. The king himself drew a double advantage from these arrangements. On the battlefields of the Silesian wars he forged a nobility proud to call itself Prussian and gave it a stake in the success of the new military absolutism. In this way the nobility lost its provincial obscurantism and identified itself with the fortunes of Frederick, giving him not merely passive obedience, but energetic support.

In France, at this period, nobles who were prevented from serving in the army or diplomatic service, usually entered the church. Such individuals in Prussia joined not the church, whose pastors were drawn exclusively from the middle-class, but the civil service. In this sphere of activity they were assured, under Frederick the Great, not only of preferential treatment, but also of a monopoly of the higher and more remunerative positions. After 1740 the ministers of the General Directory and the presidents of the War and Domain Chambers were almost invariably nobles. Under Frederick William I the nobility had, of course, been represented in the rising Prussian bureaucracy, but it had not formed the preponderant element. 'For every two nobles appointed to the provincial

Chambers', so we are told by Professor Dorn, 'the king had added two officials of bourgeois origin, to hold the balance even between the classes.' Frederick set himself, not to maintain, but to upset the balance in favour of the nobility, if not as regards mere numbers, certainly as regards the proportion holding responsible and permanent appointments. Most nobles could now count on becoming part of the permanent establishment after a short initial period of service of four to five years, whereas middle-class civil servants were only confirmed in their appointments after serving in subordinate posts for fifteen or twenty years. Cabinet councillors of middle-class origins were no longer, as under Frederick William I, promoted to ministerial rank, and the only exception to this rule was the appointment of Michaelis as minister responsible for the government of the Electoral Mark and Postmaster-General. It is fair to add, however, that all the nobles who entered the civil service had graduated at one or other of the four Prussian universities, had won their appointments by examination and had undergone a period of careful technical preparation. A further justification of this system was that, until 1807, the middle-class callings and liberal professions, as well as trade and industry, remained closed to the nobility, partly by custom and partly as a result of governmental regulations. There were, moreover, few, if any, sinecures in the administration of Frederick the Great. The moral discipline, personal self-sacrifice and devotion to duty which were characteristic of the higher branches of the Prussian civil service in the eighteenth century owed not a little to this infusion of aristocratic influence.

The king also called a halt to the anti-feudal policy of his predecessors in the sphere of local government. Except in Silesia and West Prussia, where Frederick was eager to undermine the political influence of the former Austrian and Polish nobilities, no further inroads were made on the powers of the provincial diets or *Landtage*. The attempt of Frederick William I to convert the *Landräte* into purely bureaucratic agents of the central power was abandoned. Under the general supervision of the War and Domain Chambers, the noble *Landräte* remained vested with a bewildering variety of local administrative tasks which made their position reminiscent of the English Justices of the Peace, except that they had no judicial authority and were paid partly by the Treasury and partly by the local estates. These officials controlled the activities of a number of local dignitaries, who were themselves noble – dyke-captains, directors of poor-relief and inspectors of fire-prevention societies. If it be remembered that the nobles also exercised rights of private jurisdiction on their manorial estates and collected the *Kontribution*, or main direct tax, from the peasants, their responsibility for the conduct of rural local government can be seen to have been considerable.

Within the limits imposed by his Mercantilist economic policy and by his determination to conserve a prosperous peasantry for reasons of national defence, Frederick the Great also did his best to protect the interests of the nobility as owners of landed property. He abandoned his predecessor's practice of enlarging the crown domain by buying up manorial estates belonging to the nobility. Such a policy, he remarked, might benefit a Prince of Zippel-Zerbst, but not the king of Prussia. He stopped legal proceedings whose object was to recover crown lands from the nobility. Nor did he attempt to disturb the existing feudal and economic relations of the lords with their peasants, except to punish arbitrary and harsh treatment of the tenants and to stop their eviction by engrossing landholders. More significant were three positive measures which the king took to preserve the economic independence of the nobility as landed proprietors. The first of these was the effort to uphold the noble monopoly of manorial estates or *Rittergüter*. Believing, as a matter of general principle, that the middle-class should invest its free capital in commerce and industry, Frederick repeatedly forbade the sale of noble land (*adelige Güter*) to non-noble prospective purchasers, unless with his express consent. This embargo was not applied to small

properties of from ten to twenty hides, or in Silesia and West
Prussia. Nor, for a variety of reasons which will be explained
later, did it prevent the middle-class from acquiring noble land
exceptionally. Where this happened, however, middle-class
investors were precluded from acquiring the normal feudal
rights enjoyed by lords of the manor; they were explicitly
debarred from exercising rights of private jurisdiction, from
acting as lay patrons, and from participating in meetings of the
provincial or local estates. After 1762 such owners were forbidden to resell noble land to middle-class purchasers, and
after 1775 from leaving it by will to middle-class descendants.
The second measure taken by Frederick was the encouragement
given to owners of manorial property to restrict inheritance
claims on their landed estates by means of *Fideikommisse*. The
advantages of such family instruments were considerable. In
the absence of any system of primogeniture, they restricted
the succession to a single son or single agnate, leaving other
descendants, male or female, to be provided for by cash
settlements. They also secured to the existing landowner the
independent administration of the estate, thus freeing him from
the interference and hampering control of expectant legatees.
Lastly, they prevented the alienation, but not necessarily the
mortgaging, of the family estates. In April 1754 the king
despatched a cabinet order addressed to the nobility recom-
mending the formation of such entails as a means of conserving
manorial property. In 1765 a royal circular was also addressed
to the highest judicial tribunals of the provinces – the *Regie-
rungen* – repeating the advice with greater insistence, and to this
policy the dynasty adhered till the downfall of the *Ancien
Régime* in 1807. Thirdly, in order to compensate the nobility
for its sacrifices in blood and material possessions during the
Seven Years War, Frederick encouraged the formation, especially in the distressed areas, of rural credit institutions, which
were prepared to facilitate long-term mortgage loans at low
rates of interest to embarrassed noble proprietors. During the
war many noble families had been decimated, estates had been

left to decay or had been fought over and laid waste. The restriction on the sale of noble land to the middle-class, which had been temporarily lifted during the war, was reimposed at its close and this had a depressing effect on land prices. Acting on suggestions made to him by a Berlin merchant named Büring, Frederick had founded a mortgage institute in Silesia in 1770, and this model was copied with modifications by the Electoral Mark in 1777 and by Pomerania in 1780. These institutions were subsidized by generous grants from the central government, for though Prussia itself had been financially exhausted by the war, the resources of the royal treasury were still intact. None of these initiatives succeeded and it is important to understand why they failed.

The first reason must be sought in the reluctance of many of the Prussian manorial estate owners at this period to abandon the feudal inheritance restrictions concerning the transmission of landed property. This attitude was shaped by two governing principles. The first of these was the commonly recognized obligation of existing owners not to alienate or mortgage their estates in an irresponsible manner, since these were regarded as the property, not of an individual, but of the family, of the born and unborn alike. The second principle was that all the sons of a feudal tenant, or, in default of sons, all the male members of the family who stood nearest to him in degree of relationship, had equal inheritance claims on the estate, and should, if possible, be endowed with some landed property. Though these principles were found, in practice, to conflict with each other, the nobility as a class could not bring itself to surrender either of them. Once the actual inheritor of the estate had been decided by mutual agreement or even by lot, it then remained to satisfy the claims of the co-heirs by the division of the property, or by money settlements. Before this happened, provision had also to be made for the female dependants of the deceased. Cash dowries for the daughters and allowances for the widows thus caused a considerable financial drain on the estates of the Prussian nobility. In default

of direct heirs, disagreements among the residuary male legatees, moreover, frequently gave rise to endless family disputes
and litigation. Under this system the real threat to family
holdings came not from their subdivision, for this usually
happened only in the case of very large properties, but from
the necessity of encumbering the estates with debt in order to
meet cash settlements or allowances. Alienation of part of the
properties, or the raising of loans, however, met with a serious
obstacle in another characteristic feature of feudal property law
in Prussia – the requirement of the previous consent of the
agnates, i.e. of all the male descendants of the common ancestor,
who had originally brought the fief into the family. These
restrictions on the transmission of manorial estates arising out
of the feudal nexus (*Lehnsverband*) were admittedly becoming
obsolete in the eighteenth century, and some Prussian nobles
refused to be bound by them. Others, nevertheless, adhered to
them and, consequently, found themselves in serious economic
difficulties in the second half of the century. The conversion of
manorial estates into *Fideikommisse*, as recommended by the
crown, would undoubtedly have eased the burden of indebted-
ness, but the nobility did not resort to this remedy on an
adequate scale until after 1807. Till the end of the *Ancien Régime*
the Prussian nobility continued steadfast in its conviction that
all the family dependants of the feudal tenant could and should
be provided for out of the inheritance.

In the last quarter of the century, however, the primary
need of the Prussian landholding class was for an efficient
system of obtaining long-term credit on reasonable terms.
This was needed, not only in order to meet inheritance claims,
but also to tide estate owners over the severe economic crisis
after the Seven Years War and to allow them to adopt the
more costly methods of scientific agriculture. The solution to
the problem might, conceivably, have been found in the
mortgage credit institutions devised by Frederick, but the
whole situation was bedevilled by the increasing insistence on
the necessity of obtaining the consent of the agnates before

mortgage loans were contracted. A feudal constitution elaborated by the dynasty in 1723 had, it is true, attempted to overcome this difficulty by providing that, where nobles wished to raise money on their estates to provide for their female dependants, or in order to carry out 'useful improvements' to their property, the consent of the agnates should not be withheld. This relaxation, however, was not adequate to meet the situation which arose in the 'seventies. It did not, for example, envisage the possibility that a prolonged economic crisis might compel landed proprietors to mortgage their estates out of sheer necessity. Nor could it prevent lenders, in times of stringency, from insisting on the consent of the agnates in order to increase the security of their loans. Once the movement for scientific farming had developed, the agnates themselves often felt obliged to put a restrictive interpretation on the term 'useful improvement', and to withhold their consent to loans sought by progressive landholders. A further attempt was therefore made to circumvent these difficulties by a numerous group of nobles in the Electoral Mark at the time of the foundation of the mortgage institutes. It was now suggested that for future loans the prior consent of the nearest five agnates should suffice and that, in the case of loans which had been irregularly contracted in the past, the necessity for consent should be remitted. The opposition of a strongly organized minority, however, defeated these projects. The whole basis of the new credit institutes was that mortgages should receive the collective guarantee of the members. Yet landowners who could not contract loans on their own authority could hardly guarantee loans raised by other borrowers. It was this fundamental difficulty which prevented the mortgage institutes from functioning effectively. The substitution of long-term for short-term mortgages thus became impossible and frequent foreclosures during the economic troubles of the 'seventies involved the alienation of many noble estates.

For these reasons the Prussian nobility was being steadily driven to liquidate portions of its landed possessions. As the century drew to its close this tendency was strengthened by a rise in land values. This induced the successors of Frederick II to connive at the sale of manorial property to the middle-class, in order that the nobility could profit from the improved economic situation. Some 'concealed' sales occurred through noble intermediaries, others took the form of hereditary or long leases granted by officers and civil servants whose duties prevented them from administering their estates in person. On the whole, it was the smaller rather than the larger properties which came into the market, though many of the older families, such as the von Winterfelds, the von Rohrs, the von Krosigks, indulged in land speculation. The middle-class and even the peasants were eager purchasers, for the acquisition of 'noble' land carried with it, if not full manorial rights, at all events freedom from taxation or emancipation from feudal labour services. It has been calculated that, in 1800, 9 per cent of the proprietors of noble estates in the Electoral Mark (exclusive of the Old Mark) were middle-class, and that in the four districts of Uckermark, Niederbarnim, Lebus and Ruppin, middle-class proprietors held approximately 5 per cent of the total value of the manorial estates. These figures indicate the extent to which the embargo on sales to the middle-class had been disregarded, at least in the central provinces of Prussia.

After the death of Frederick II the nobility thus became more and more dependent for their livelihood upon careers in the public service, although experience had already shown that this could provide only inadequate support. The extent of that dependence may be judged from the returns of the *Vassallenta-belle* of the Electoral Mark in 1800, which showed that three-quarters of the landed proprietors in the area had served, at one time or another, in the army or civil service. Except in the higher ranges of the civil administration, however, salaries were only moderate, and, as the century advanced, increasing numbers of nobles were compelled to occupy even minor and poorly paid administrative posts as excise officers, cemetery inspectors and surveyors. Throughout the century the pay of army officers was miserable, so that married officers without private means had no prospect of educating their children, except in the state cadet schools founded by Frederick the Great. Charitable schemes had also to be organized for the benefit of officers' widows and daughters. The Prussian nobility was, in fact, already too numerous to be supported by their official salaries. Part of the trouble was that landless nobles were less inclined than they had previously been to surrender their titles and social status in order to recruit their fortunes by adopting middle-class occupations. Frederick, indeed, had placed a premium on the readoption of noble status in the civil service, and the result was that many non-nobles who claimed descent from noble stock, took steps to reacquire their titles – especially in the period 1786-94. The ranks of the nobility were also swollen by the incorporation of Polish nobles after 1772 and by French émigrés after 1789. The main source of the increase, however, was new creations in the reign of Frederick William II (1786-97). Allowing for the difference in the length of their reigns, Frederick William II created five times as many nobles as Frederick the Great, who himself had created twice as many as Frederick William I. Though the rate slackened after 1797, it was still twice as great under Frederick William III as it had been in the first half of the eighteenth century. The reaction of the older nobility was to seek promotion to the rank of baron, count, or even prince. These elevations were usually hedged about with restrictions, princely titles being confined to eldest sons and the rank of count being often granted for life only. This proliferation of the nobility in the latter years of the century drew sharp criticism not only from those who wished to destroy, but also from those who wished to defend, aristocratic privileges. In the end it rendered the caste system of Frederick the Great ridiculous.

The solution which Stein and the liberal reformers found for this impoverishment of the Prussian nobility was, indeed, to break down the existing social barriers by the law of 9th

October 1807. This legislation opened up to the nobility access to the liberal professions and to trade and industry without involving it thereby in the loss of its pretensions to noble status, and permitted the acquisition of manorial estates by the middle-class without conferring on purchasers recognition as nobles. As a result, in place of the old estate of nobility, there arose in Prussia in the nineteenth century new social groups in which noble and bourgeois freely intermingled. Aristocratic monopolies disappeared, though traces of the feudal nexus lingered on, the peasants were emancipated and the Junkers of East Prussia took on a new lease of life as large-scale capitalist farmers. The poverty-stricken nobles continued to be a social problem, but the nobility as a whole was free not only to play an important part in the emancipation of Prussia from the tutelage of Napoleon, but to enter on a new stage of its existence in the nineteenth century with better prospects of restoring its dwindling economic revenues and with a restored sense of its ability to serve the Prussian state.

6

AUSTRIA

H. G. Schenk

THE subject of this essay is the Austrian nobility in the wider
sense of the term 'Austrian'; that is to say, the region covered
will consist not only of the hereditary Habsburg possessions
proper, but also of the lands of the Crown of Bohemia, namely
that country itself, Moravia and Silesia. The Magyar nobility, in
many aspects substantially different, will be touched upon only
in so far as they made themselves conspicuous in Austria proper.
In time my range will be the eighteenth century up to the
death of Emperor Joseph II in 1790, but once or twice, especially in my discussion of the state of affairs in Bohemia, reference
will be made to the seventeenth century. Both higher and
lower nobility will be included. The dividing line between the
two separated the counts who were subject to the Emperor
alone, *reichsunmittelbare Grafen*, from an inferior group of
counts who did not share this privilege. In the lower category
were also included the Imperial barons and all the other barons
or *Freiherren*. Throughout the Holy Roman Empire the higher
nobility was also distinguished by the privilege of a seat and a
vote in the *Reichstag* at Ratisbon.

If the nobility in eighteenth-century England held power
without privileges, and the reverse be true of France, the
Austrian nobility at the beginning of the eighteenth century
and almost up to the middle of it can be said to have held both:
power and privileges, or, at any rate, a considerable measure
of power and very wide privileges. The nobility's main source
of wealth lay in its landed estates; except for the sovereign, no

stratum of society could even hope to compete with the nobility's wealth, much less with that of the richest noble families such as the Esterházis in Hungary, the Schwarzenbergs in Austria or the Lobkowitzes in Bohemia. It has been calculated that in Moravia, for example, one-third of the soil lay in the hands of the nobility. In Austria, as in England, there existed a strong desire on the part of aristocratic landowners to keep the family estate intact. The means of achieving this end consisted in the so-called *Fideikommiss*, a kind of land-trust holding, far more rigorous than the elastic system prevailing in England. It is now believed that the legal concept of the *Fideikommiss* had come to Austria from Spain round about 1600; Italian jurists had perfected it. For the establishment of a *Fideikommiss* the sovereign's authorization was required, as a rule. In the vast majority of cases it was coupled with the age-old institution of primogeniture by which the whole estate in question always passed to the eldest son of the eldest line. In some circumstances, for example where there was no male heir, the eldest daughter could succeed to the estate if the founder so wished. The *Fideikommiss*, which could be established also in the form of a testament, secured the family estate against alienation as well as against substantial mortgaging. For certain purposes and within certain limits the estate could be mortgaged. Never under any circumstances was the ownership to be transferred to another family. Yet economic forces and the vagaries of human nature are at times stronger than the most stringent law, and thus it happened after all that *Fideikommiss* estates were sold, with the authorization of the sovereign, in order that family debts, incurred through extravagance or heavy tax arrears, could be paid off.

We have seen that the eldest son was, as a rule, extremely well provided for. What about the other children? – often there were many of them; the famous Kaunitz, for example, was one of fifteen, which was not altogether exceptional. Several chances offered themselves. Service at the Imperial Court had been considerably expanded towards the end of the seventeenth century, no doubt in emulation of the dazzling court of Louis XIV. When, in 1703, the brother of Emperor Joseph I, the pompous Prince Charles, visited England on his way to Spain, he brought with him a retinue of 164 persons, 210 horses and 47 carriages. When some eight years later the Prince became the Emperor Charles VI, his court, according to a contemporary estimate, consisted of no less than 40,000 persons, numerous leading positions being, of course, in the hands of the nobility. Most of them served, officially, for the sake of the honour only, which must have made certain considerable perquisites that accrued to them all the more welcome. Thus every newly appointed chamberlain had to pay to the lord chamberlain a round sum of 200 ducats. Count Trautson, we are told, received in 1709 from the Emperor, as a handsome present for Easter Day, a creation of 300 new chamberlains. At the death of Maria Theresa there existed nearly 1500 chamberlains. The great feudal offices, that of Lord Chamberlain, Lord Steward, etc., were either left vacant or were suppressed by Joseph II. Other offices, such as the newly created *Erblandfalkenmeister*, falconer of the hereditary lands, were nothing but empty titles, but served at any rate to increase the social prestige of some noble families, as for example the Thürheims, Lambergs and Kufsteins. Apart from court service itself, there existed all kinds of openings in the service of the crown. In 1705, at the death of Leopold I, there were thirteen ministers (*Konferenzräte*) and 164 privy councillors (*Geheimräte*) all of whom belonged to the higher nobility. We are not precisely informed about the salaries and other benefits attached to these high offices; it seems, however, that they compared unfavourably with analogous positions in England. This was at any rate the impression gathered by Sir Nathaniel Wraxall who visited Vienna in 1779.

Further openings, and a good many of them, offered themselves in the army. Poorer nobles, including younger brothers of very rich nobles, flocked to the Austrian standards gladly accepting commissions in his Imperial Majesty's service. War proved to be a fairly constant employer throughout the best part of the century, though warfare itself was on the whole not as ruthless as during the preceding age of religious wars or the subsequent period of nationalist wars. One more source of income has to be mentioned here, namely, ecclesiastical sinecures which Austrian aristocrats exploited hardly less than their French compeers. Kaunitz, himself a younger son, was awarded by the Pope the vacant prebend of Münster in Westphalia even before the prescribed minimum age of fourteen.

For the unmarried daughters of higher noble families there existed foundations such as the *Sternkreuzorden*, a religious order instituted by the Empress Eleonore in 1668, or the more recent semi-religious Savoy foundation for noble ladies, endowed by Princess Liechtenstein in Vienna in 1769. Ladies wishing to leave the last-mentioned institution in order to get married even received a dowry from the funds of the foundation. In spite of all this, there remained a certain number of unmarried noble ladies in reduced financial circumstances.

Unlike England, the nobility's income was not supplemented by appreciable commercial or industrial ventures. In industry Counts Harrach and Kinsky formed the exception that proved the rule. When Baron Fuchs who had done well in commerce was made Count in 1781, Joseph II significantly added the rider that the new Count and his sons should continue in commerce, as the Emperor did not regard big commercial enterprise as being beneath the dignity of the high nobility. Since no other section of the population excelled in these pursuits, the position of the nobility was at least not seriously threatened from below; unlike England, Austria did not possess a plutocracy at this period. This is one of the reasons why it is impossible to compare the economic power of the Austrian nobles with that of their compeers in this country; but even if we were to base our comparison upon the criterion of landed possessions alone, when at first sight the Austrian nobles would come out very well, we should have to remember that under the prevailing system of feudalism the land in Austria would not yield as much as in England where, by then, a more advanced agricultural system had come to be adopted.

Inside the ranks of the nobility the lower nobility continued to look up to their social superiors. To use Professor Arnold Toynbee's terminology: their attitude, at any rate until the middle of the century, was characterized by social imitation or mimesis.

The financial position of the Austrian nobility was yet further strengthened by the fact that they were able to exploit the lands of the ancient Crown of Bohemia, or at any rate, very large portions of them, almost in the same manner in which other Powers exploited overseas colonies. The Protestant majority of the old Bohemian nobility had been forced into exile after the battle of the White Mountain in 1620. There remained only eight of the ancient Czech aristocratic families in these lands, namely the Czernins, Kinskys, Kolovrats, Lobkowitzes, Waldsteins, Schlicks, Sternbergs and Kaunitzes. Towards the end of the century only about 15 per cent of the nobility in these regions belonged to the old Bohemian nobility both Czech and German. Where did the other 85 per cent come from? Some, as for example the Trautmannsdorfs, Auerspergs and Sterneggs, came from various parts of Austria (including Carniola and Styria), others, like the Schwarzenbergs, Fürstenbergs and Rottenhaus, from Germany, the Bouquoys came from France, the Desfours from Lorraine, the Wallises from England, and the Taaffes, MacNevens and O'Kelleys from Ireland. All these foreign nobles or, as the case might be, adventurers had for a variety of reasons offered their services to the Emperor, and during and after the Thirty Years War they were richly rewarded. It has been rightly emphasized that the resulting denationalization of the Bohemian nobility has remained one of the decisive factors in the history of that unfortunate country. Not only was the composition of the nobility now residing in Bohemia exceedingly heterogeneous, but the very institution of a distinct Bohemian nobility was abolished by Maria Theresa in 1752. There can be no doubt that this step was taken in order to forestall a recurrence of the disaffection of 1741, when in the midst of the turmoil of the War of Austrian Succession a considerable portion of the Bohemian nobility had sworn homage to the Elector of Bavaria who was crowned King of Bohemia in December 1741. Maria Theresa, at her own coronation in Prague in 1743, could well compare the Bohemian Crown to a fool's cap.

Henceforth, that is after 1752, there was to exist only a joint Bohemian-Austrian nobility. By Haugwitz's far-reaching administrative reforms of 1749 Austria and Bohemia had been firmly welded together, and ten years later Bartenstein, in a memoir on the internal constitution of Bohemia, Moravia and Silesia, impressed upon the young Crown Prince Joseph the principle of promoting the settlement and intermarriage of the Austrian nobility in Bohemia and of the Bohemian nobility in Austria. In higher circles the Czech language, which had a proud literary record going back to the Middle Ages, was now, according to the Czech chronicler Pešina, hardly spoken at all, though such great families as the Kinskys and Sternbergs never entirely abandoned it. Obviously all these factors together resulted in an estrangement between the somewhat *déracinés* noble squires and their serfs, the majority of whom were Czech-speaking Bohemians or Moravians. Increasing absenteeism on the part of the squires, no less than the process of conglomeration of landed property by which some of the nobles (the Lobkowitzes and Schwarzenbergs for example) became land-holding magnates on a vast scale, tended to deepen the cleavage. The serf risings of 1679, and again of 1767 and 1775, provided significant pointers in this direction.

Brighter spots were not altogether lacking in this rather gloomy picture. Count Franz Anton Sporck (1662–1738), himself owner of extensive estates in North-eastern Bohemia, strongly condemned the exploitation of the lower classes. By alleviating the burden of his serfs' *Robot* (or *corvée*) duties, by generous gifts to those in need, as well as by the foundation of hospitals and other benevolent institutions, Count Sporck earned for himself the epithets 'father of the poor' and 'the noble Count', thus proving, if indeed proof were needed, that nobility in rank could well be combined with nobility of heart.

The second half of the eighteenth century was for the Habsburg Empire in general a period of integration and centralization. Imperial power, so triumphant during the Counter-reformation a century earlier, had been unable to consolidate all its gains between the Peace of Westphalia in 1648 and the Peace of Aix-la-Chapelle in 1748, mainly for two reasons. In the first place, subordinate administration had during that time still remained in the hands of the decentralized provincial diets (*Stände*), and secondly, financial embarrassment of the central power had often made necessary political concessions to the 'intermediary powers', as Montesquieu called them. In some cases, though officially no concessions were made, in point of fact decrees enacted in the name of the Emperor were flouted, especially in the all-important sphere of tax collection. The recession of the central power's authority had made itself felt particularly during the last anxious years of the régime of Charles VI. Soon afterwards fell the three blows which seemed to spell utter disaster for the dynasty: Frederic's rape of Silesia; the election of a non-Habsburg, the Elector of Bavaria, to the dignity of Emperor; finally, in 1744, Frederic's invasion of Bohemia. The wars and confusion that ensued came to a temporary standstill only in 1748. The régime of the Habsburg heiress, which Maria Theresa was now recognized to be, had almost surprisingly withstood the onslaught, though precious Silesia had to be sacrificed. But one thing had emerged quite clearly, namely that the Habsburg possessions in their present state of disorganization would not be able to weather another storm. The Ottoman menace in the sixteenth and seventeenth centuries had brought Hungary, Austria and Bohemia closer together; it was the Prussian menace that completed this process. *Fas est et ab hoste doceri* – it was the efficiency of Prussian administration in newly conquered Silesia that made the greatest impression on Count Haugwitz. The writings of the so-called *Kameralisten*, and Schroeder in particular, pointed in the same direction. Maria Theresa, advised by Haugwitz, now embarked upon far-reaching centralizing measures which to Prince Khevenhüller, the faithful Lord High Steward, seemed a total reversal of traditional Habsburg policy. However that might be, many a time-honoured institution now had to be remodelled or entirely abolished, and a modern comparatively efficient bureaucracy created. Although Prince Kaunitz in 1762 repealed some of Haugwitz's administrative reforms, the main trend was not affected. Provincialism, not only in the Bohemian lands, but also in some Austrian provinces themselves, was considerably reduced. Obviously the power and privileges of the feudal nobility now came to be curtailed though individual noblemen for a long time retained the highest position in the state, for example Kaunitz, Kolowrat, Seilern, Esterházi and Zinzendorf. But it was highly significant that Joseph II, far more critical of the nobility than his mother, appointed seven non-noble secretaries to his Imperial Cabinet. In the War ministry, during Joseph's régime, about 75 per cent of the officials did not belong to the nobility. But even where nobles often belonging to the lower nobility were appointed, for example to newly created bureaucratic posts, they henceforth became Habsburg officials first and foremost, and supported the central power in its struggle against the recalcitrant intermediary powers of nobility, clergy, guilds and so forth. Gradually under Maria Theresa, and with growing momentum under Joseph II, the state brought the lower classes explicitly within the orbit of its ordinances, and transformed those former subjects of the feudal nobility into individual citizens. In passing it may be noted that a proposal to this effect had already been put forward under Charles VI by the publicist Schierl von Schierendorff. Political, fiscal, as well as genuinely humanitarian motives were all inextricably interwoven. The upshot was: first, an early example of state intervention, namely the so-called *Robot* legislation by which the imposition of forced labour services in agriculture was confined to certain fixed limits; secondly, the abolition of serfdom on Maria Theresa's crown domains which was meant to set an example to the aristocratic squires; finally, Joseph's celebrated decree of February 1789 which abolished forced labour services altogether. The Emperor who had made so many enemies abroad as well as at home, could well say that he had no need to fear any opposition to his régime, for he could rely upon an army of 300,000 men and upon the affection of the emancipated serfs.

To recruit the large contingent of officials needed for the reorganization of the Habsburg domains was not an easy task. It was made more arduous by the fact that, proportionately, there seem to have been fewer intellectuals in Austria proper than in a corresponding area of Germany. As to the reformers themselves, Counts Haugwitz and Hatzfeld were natives of Silesia, Bartenstein hailed from Alsace, Count Chotek came from Bohemia, Kaunitz and Sonnenfels from Moravia. Maria Theresa, though typically Austrian in so many ways, had a North German Princess for her mother. The father of Joseph II was a Lorrainer. A good number of officials came from Protestant Germany and were duly ennobled in Vienna. The cosmopolitan character of the nobility in Austria was thus further intensified. True, some of the great families, as for instance the Liechtensteins, Dietrichsteins, Auerspergs, Khevenhüllers, Starhembergs and Windischgrätzs, had their roots in Austria proper; but others had come to Austria in the seventeenth century from Germany (the Stadions, Fürstenbergs, Schwarzenbergs, Salms, Schönborns), from Italy (the Colloredos, Montecucculis, Piccolominis), from Spain (the Hoyos), from Ireland (the O'Briens), from Scotland (the Ogilvys). Many of these had offered their sword to the cause of the Habsburgs, and again towards the end of the seventeenth and during the eighteenth centuries the Habsburgs were fortunate enough to secure the services of such great soldiers as Prince Eugene of Savoy, Laudon who came from Livonia (though he was of Scottish descent), Daun a native of the Rhineland, and last but not least the spirited Irishman O'Donnell who during the Seven Years War received the Maria Theresa Order for an extremely daring exploit. Often these men had held foreign titles which were sooner or later recognized and, as it were, naturalized.

This multinational society used French as their *lingua franca*, especially since the accession of Maria Theresa. But Italian too, the first language under Charles VI, was still widely understood; Metastasio, court poet from 1729, wrote in Italian, and the Capuchin friar Caslino used the same language for his sermons at St. Peter's Church, Vienna, as late as 1748. Towards the end of the century the English travellers Henry Swinburne and Sir Nathaniel Wraxall reported that the noble ladies in Vienna spoke English fairly well. When we consider that German too was, of course, spoken or understood by most members of the higher classes, we get the picture of a linguistic accomplishment not equalled by the nobility in any other eighteenth-century capital, or indeed, one might almost say, at any time, with the one exception of the Russian aristocracy described in Tolstoi's novels. With the knowledge of three or four European languages there was sometimes combined a wider European outlook which in more recent times has become all but extinct.

Ennoblements were fairly frequent in eighteenth-century Austria. Agents who could pull a few strings were employed in the process. The musician Dittersdorf paid his agent fifty ducats, but the patent of nobility itself cost him over 1000 florins. Among those newly ennobled were confidential post-masters in charge of post-lodges, secret offices, that is, intercepting letters. Metternich's second wife, Antonia von Leykam, belonged to a family of such postal upstarts. An interesting case of recent ennoblement was that of Baron von Sonnenfels's father. He was an eminent scholar of Semitic languages, himself a Jew by the name of Lipman Perlin and son of a Berlin rabbi. While in Nikolsburg in Southern Moravia he came in touch with priests whom he taught Hebrew, and gained the favour and support of Charles Prince Dietrichstein. He became a convert to Christianity, changed his name, had both his sons baptized, though his wife clung to her Jewish faith, moved to Vienna where in 1745 he was appointed to a teaching post at the University, and a year later received the cherished patent of nobility. Racial anti-Semitism, that modern abomination, had yet to be invented, and thus the way lay open for Josef von Sonnenfels whose main claim to fame was the part he later played in the abolition of torture. Enlightened reform of criminal procedure, fervently advocated by the Italian jurist Beccaria, was thus adopted in Austria. As editor of the weekly periodical *Der Mann ohne Vorurteil* (The Man without Prejudice) Sonnenfels attacked, often successfully, a variety of other inveterate abuses. In 1797 he became a baron.

The conversion of Sonnenfels's father was not exceptional. It is invidious to throw doubt upon the genuineness of a particular conversion, but when we read of a whole series of German Protestants (e.g. Prince Hildburghausen, Count Haugwitz, von Bartenstein, von Knorr, von Metsch, von Wurmbrand, von Wucherer) who moved to Vienna, became converts to Catholicism and then proceeded to make a career in the service of the Habsburgs, it would be naïve not to suspect their motives. It is hard not to believe that these pseudo-conversions were but symptoms of a general debasement of religion which eighteenth-century Austria experienced, though not to the same degree as France. Another symptom could be seen in the growing class-consciousness of the Church in Austria at a time when special religious orders exclusively for noble ladies were established, as for example the *Sternkreuzorden* founded in 1668 or the *Savoyische adelige Damenstift* of 1769. Similar tendencies prevailed in the cathedral chapters of Salzburg, Trient and Brixen. In spite of Papal bulls against Freemasons, issued in 1738 and again in 1751, lodges existed in eighteenth-century Vienna, Prague and a few other places, their membership consisting largely of nobility and military men. Meetings seem to have been held surreptitiously, although, on the other hand, no less august a person than Maria Theresa's husband, who was one of their members, helped his fellow-masons when, in 1743, they had difficulties with the police. Prince Kaunitz was often referred to as *il ministro eretico*; certainly not without justification. It is against this background that the large-scale secularizing measures enacted by Joseph II must be viewed.

An attempt to conjure up the atmosphere of the nobility's life and culture would be greatly aided by a visit to some aristocratic houses – *palais* as they were called in Austria. But whereas Blenheim Palace is only a bus-ride from Oxford, Vienna – let alone Prague – is, alas, not so easily accessible in present-day circumstances and most of us must therefore be satisfied with the pictorial image. In Vienna, the first big city in Central Europe (at a time when that area on the map really existed as a region!), the most representative aristocratic houses of the Baroque period are the *palais* Schwarzenberg, Kinsky and Pallavicini. A number of Austrian nobles also resided at Innsbruck, Linz and Klagenfurt, unless they preferred to live in Prague, which in architecture and scenery could rival the Imperial capital. Lady Mary Wortley Montagu reported in 1716 that people of quality, who could not easily bear the expense of Vienna, chose to reside in Prague. Besides, there was still something of the air of a capital about that city which a hundred years back had been the residence of Emperor Rudolf II. In eighteenth-century Prague the typical setting would be provided by the *palais* Czernin, Lobkowitz and Fürstenberg, as well as by the delightful gardens surrounding those splendid town residences. On the outskirts of the city, Count Michna's miniature Villa Amerika, designed by that great architect Kilian Ignaz Dientzenhofer, and Count Sternberg's picturesque Castle Troja, deserve more than a passing notice. The Magyar nobility assembled chiefly in Buda-Pest and Pressburg, but in Maria Theresa's time some prominent Magyar aristocrats came to live in Vienna or in the neighbourhood of the court. Just as in the case of Bohemia, the Magyars, for example the Esterházis, Pálffys and Batthyánys, began to intermarry with Austrian noble families. A certain number of nobles from Lombardy and the Netherlands also resided in Vienna. Besides the city *palais*, the nobility possessed country houses at Laxenburg, Dornbach and other attractive places. On their own country estates new gardens were laid out, for instance by Kaunitz at Austerlitz in Moravia. Kaunitz's garden was especially renowned for its beautiful covered colonnades. During the game-hunting season country residences, surrounded as many of them were by thick forests, became favourite meeting places of the nobility.

A young nobleman might study at the universities of Vienna or Prague, or even Paris or Padua, unless he wished to visit a German university outside the Habsburg possessions. Kaunitz chose Leipsic. In Vienna the noble might be educated at an academy specially designed for his class, such as the *Savoyische Ritterakademie* founded by Princess Liechtenstein in 1749 or the Theresian Academy founded by the Empress three years earlier. Here he would prepare for a career in the diplomatic or civil service. Education, until the 1750's largely in the hands of the clergy and the Jesuit Order in particular, was laicized and centralized. The *grand tour*, so characteristic a part of a young nobleman's education in the first half of the century, tended to disappear under the more austere state-bound régime of Joseph II. Kaunitz, at the age of twenty-two, had been sent to Germany, the Netherlands, Italy and Paris to broaden his horizon, and he met eminent statesmen, such as Cardinal Fleury, numerous artists, especially musicians, and dancers – of both sexes.

Especially at the beginning of the century, aristocratic marriages were often concluded at an early age; Kaunitz's mother was thirteen when she married. As in England, marriages were arranged, but unlike this country the sovereign (Charles VI) sometimes refused to grant the necessary permission. If marriages were arranged for prudential reasons, *liaisons*, a recognized institution, were chosen from a more personal angle; yet even they remained confined within the same stratum of society. Foreign travellers remarked on the dignified and graceful deportment of the noble ladies in Vienna, and generally on their social accomplishments. Female observers, always more severe on their own sex, did not fail to ridicule the excessively wide whalebone petticoats 'covering some acres of ground'. Evening parties and festivals of various kinds were very much *en vogue*, piquet and other card games being played by the old, while the young and those who wished to be so regarded indulged in dancing. At a *bal masqué* at court only the higher nobility were allowed to remain masked, while the others had to unmask on arrival. The Frenchman Dutens, who in the early 1780's published a kind of Baedeker, took part in a masqued ball given by Maria Theresa at the Belvedere. There were 18,000 wax-lights within the palace walls; seven thousand persons assembled. The whole festivity was conducted without the least disorder or mishap, for, as Dutens states admiringly, physicians, surgeons, midwives and beds were prepared in case of accidents – thus almost exceeding modern Welfare State standards! A favourite outdoor winter festival was described by the Englishman Wraxall; several hundred carts were employed on the preceding day to bring snow into the city and to scatter it through the principal streets, as otherwise the sledges could not be driven with ease or safety. The procession of sledges was held alternatively in day-time or by torch-light at night. It was begun by the Master of the Horse, followed by Archdukes and Archduchesses, and noblemen and women in thirty sledges; the ladies dressed in furs richly ornamented, their heads covered with jewels. The sledges themselves were gilt and carved with great taste, representing the figures of dragons, serpents, peacocks or monsters; before each ran footmen carrying long poles in their hands. Even the horses were quite obscured under the multiplicity of trappings, plumes and ornaments. The spectacle moved with amazing velocity through all the principal streets of Vienna and finished at the Imperial palace.

To return to indoor pleasures, the nobility certainly did not scorn a cultured *cuisine* and a choice of different wines that greatly impressed Lady Mary Wortley Montagu. Though *gourmands* and excessive drinkers were not unknown, the picture of sybaritic Vienna drawn in the eighteenth century by prim and unappreciative Northern Germans was grossly exaggerated. A more impartial observer, the globe-trotter Georg Forster, writing from Vienna in 1784, noted that since people ate very little in the morning or evening, dinner, which was served at about half-past two in the afternoon, had of course to be more substantial.

Of eccentrics, so conspicuous in eighteenth-century France and not even entirely unknown this side of the Channel, only one or two Austrian specimens may be mentioned. The old Prince of Saxe Hildburghausen always retired to his rest at eight o'clock, and as he walked from the *salon* to his bedchamber, he had men posted to pull off his wig and clothes, so that he was ready for his bed by the time he reached the door of his bedchamber. Prince Kaunitz of course, was a past-master in eccentricity, covering himself, as he did, with a number of black silk cloaks, varying from one to nine, just as the weather might require, shunning the slightest breeze of fresh air, cleansing his teeth and gums after dinner in front of all his guests with the most elaborate set of instruments to the accompaniment of weird noises. Whatever could remind him of illness or death had to be carefully concealed; to an old aunt of his he once sent from his table one of her favourite cakes – four years after her death! Perhaps following the lead given by the English – sport to neutralize the effects of alcohol – he made a special point of riding for an hour day in, day out, of course in an indoor riding-school. On the whole, the eccentricities of the Austrian nobility were probably more studied and less perverse than those of the French.

In the theatre, the boxes were reserved for the aristocracy, so was a certain part of the pit, the so-called *parterre noble*. According to the English music expert Dr Charles Burney, who visited Vienna in the early 1770's, the audience at concerts was often composed only of the higher strata. But, unlike religion, music commanded their genuine and whole-hearted enthusiasm. Those who could afford it had their own band and singers; some, as for example Prince Ferdinand Philipp Lobkowitz, were composers in their own right; others, especially ladies, played the harpsichord and later the piano with a remarkable degree of proficiency, or cultivated chamber music and singing; but it was as patrons of great and sometimes immortal music that Austrian noblemen and women will be remembered longest. Several names suggest themselves, of which we might select that of Countess Wilhelmine Thun, *née* Uhlefeldt, who was according to all accounts, which for once are in surprising harmony, a most charming, musical and cultured lady and patroness of Mozart during his most creative period. Gluck, Haydn, Mozart and, later, Beethoven all had their Austrian aristocratic patrons who thus helped to make Vienna the celebrated capital of music, a distinction that city was to retain for well over a century.

The even more ambitious plan of Leibniz, who, in 1704, had proposed to the Emperor Leopold I the establishment of an Academy of Sciences that Vienna might become the centre of German intellectual life, never came to fruition. In this respect, it seems, the creative power of the Austrian nobility was already spent and other social strata had not yet challenged its intellectual and political leadership, as they were doing in Prussia and other parts of Germany.

7

HUNGARY

C. A. Macartney

In 1711 the fighting which had been going on intermittently for many years between the Imperial forces and those of a long series of Hungarian national leaders was brought to a close by the Peace of Szatmár. Itself an armistice rather than a peace – for it provided for little more than the cessation of hostilities and amnesty in favour of the 'national' party – this instrument was admittedly concluded as the prelude to a general settlement between the two parties: the dynasty and the Hungarian nation.

The word 'nation' is used here in a technical sense of a body which sometimes used that word as its own official designation; sometimes the formula 'barons, prelates and nobles of Hungary', and sometimes – since prelates and barons were only nobles of a higher estate – simply 'universal nobility of Hungary'. It was a highly peculiar body, whose position in 1711, its claim to be entitled to negotiate with its crowned king as one contracting party with another, and the nature of the demands which it was to put forward at the negotiations, derived – as its own representatives regularly asserted – from the very origins of the Hungarian monarchy, and cannot be truly appreciated without reference to those origins.

In the year A.D. 1000 Stephen, son of Géza, hereditary supreme leader of a tent-dwelling warrior-herdsman community which, a century earlier still, had moved its quarters *en masse* from the Pontic steppes to the then almost unpeopled basin of the Middle Danube, had, as part of a somewhat complex political transaction, received from Pope Sylvester II a royal crown, in return for which he had undertaken to enforce on his followers, now to be his subjects in the fuller sense which would derive from his own changed status, the Christian faith which was already his own. The Hungarian people had, before that time, admitted no such authority over themselves as was now envisaged. They were a community the essence of whose existence was that every member of it was free (there were slaves attached to it but they simply did not count in the constitutional picture, any more than the flocks and herds) and all equal, with the single qualification that on the call to war and in the conduct of it they obeyed hereditary leaders, of whom the chief had been Stephen's ancestors; but the few decisions which affected their corporate existence were taken by themselves in conclave. Had they been acquainted with modern terminology, they would certainly have maintained themselves to be a sovereign people whose sovereign will was expressed in conclave.

The people could not entirely resist Stephen's claim, reinforced as it was by the presence of heavily-armoured German knights. But this by no means meant that they were prepared to exchange their status of free men for one of unconditional subjection, nor to abrogate completely or for ever their sovereign right of disposing of their own destinies. Thus what now took place was not an act of submission, but what may fairly be described as a grand constitutional settlement. While accepting monarchy as their permanent form of government and Stephen and his heirs male, until the extinction of the line, as monarchs, the nation yet reserved to its members and their descendants the right of electing their own monarch when Stephen's line died out, thus asserting its continued existence as a political entity and even, it may be said, its ultimate sovereignty. Even under the hereditary monarchy it remained a partner in the state; and an effective one. Even if it allowed the monarchic authority to be absolute except where limited by specific enactment, mutually agreed, it yet laid down limitations which were very far-reaching. Whether Stephen bound himself to accept the opinion of his councillors outside these limits is uncertain; but the nation certainly stipulated for itself and its members for ever certain cardinal rights and liberties which no legislation might override and no action contravene. No member of the 'nation' could be subject to any other, except only to the king, acting personally or through his appointed representatives. Their personal liberty was inviolable except for certain flagrant cases, and their status inalienable except for certain proved crimes which carried with them the penalty of exclusion from the privileged community. They had the right of direct access to the king's justice. They were bound to follow the king's call to war, but owed to the state no other service or due. In consequence, their lands, which were now allotted to them inalienably, and with free right of testamentary and other disposition over them, were tax free. Land not so allotted was taken as its property by the crown, whose officials administered it and exacted from its cultivators the taxation which was their contribution to the state, as military service was that of the freemen.

As Stephen's rights passed to his son's sons, so these rights and privileges, secured for their own persons and property by the 'nation' of his day, passed to their sons' sons in perpetuity; and it goes without saying that they were to continue to be the prerogatives of a privileged community. Not only would it have seemed psychologically absurd to these proud warriors to place slaves and subjected peasants on an equal footing with themselves, but to do so would have undermined the whole economic basis of their existence. Even to allow the inhabitants of the crown lands, over whom they had no direct control, equality with themselves would have taken most of the psychological and much of the economic value from their own status; nor, reasons of national sentiment apart (and Stephen was a Magyar himself), could the crown, which needed taxes as well as soldiers, have afforded to extend to the whole population of Hungary what it allowed to the 'nation'. Yet it was impossible to exclude all possibility of recruitment to the ranks of the military class, and although the early documents give no clear indication of any specific agreement on this all-important point, it is certain that Stephen himself conferred what later came to be known as Hungarian 'nobility' on some of his foreign helpers; and that some early immigrants entering Hungary were recognized as 'noble' and at once took their places as such among the members of the 'nation'; while later theory laid it down that the king, as the fountain of nobility, could ennoble whom he would, unless to do so would somehow have infringed an existing right.[1]

Finally, since the land of Hungary was at once the king's and the nation's, each was bound to defend it for the other. As a noble could not rebel or secede, so the king could not cede any part of it, or place it under any other form of government.

To pass immediately from the eleventh to the eighteenth century may seem abrupt, but the essential of the Hungarian nation's claim at Szatmár was that it was entitled to precisely that status and those rights which had been agreed seven hundred years earlier. It was still the coexistent and co-perpetual partner with the monarch in the Hungarian State, a thesis not invented but formulated in the sixteenth century by the jurist Wérböczy in the doctrine of the mystic unity of the Holy Crown, of which the king, fountain of nobility (i.e. membership of the 'nation') and the noble community, fountain of kingship, were the mutually complementary and mutually dependent 'members'. It still had the right to determine the succession to the throne on the lapse of any special agreements, which at that date meant, when the male line of Leopold I of Habsburg died out (it having, under great pressure, consented in 1687 to accept the hereditary accession of the Habsburgs, as so limited). Meanwhile, such adjustments of the terms of the partnership as either party to it wished to demand,

---

[1] This summary description necessarily passes over many points of detail: the distinction which long existed, but ultimately disappeared, between the status of land 'noble' in virtue of original occupation and that donated with conferred nobility; nobility acquired by adoption, delegation, etc., etc.

or decisions arising out of those terms, were discussed between the partners (king and nation) at meetings which in time had taken the form of a regular Diet. The personal rights and prerogatives which the nation consistently claimed for its members were, with slight modifications, exactly those for which it had stipulated in A.D. 1000. And as in A.D. 1000, those rights were those of the 'nation' and the 'nation' alone. Hungary's non-noble population was no longer enslaved and its members were entitled to such protection as Christian doctrine declared to be the due of all men. But they were and remained, as Wérböczy put it pithily, the 'misera contribuens plebs'. They could not own Hungarian land nor have any voice in the affairs of the nation. This principle was qualified only in so far as the Royal Free Boroughs were given some representation by the device of giving, not each citizen, but each borough, the status of a Hungarian noble.

It remains to say what were the differences both in the composition of the nation itself and in the circumstances surrounding it which made a settlement concluded between Charles III and the Hungarian nation of 1711 really something different, even if its terms were identical, from one between St. Stephen and the nation of A.D. 1000.

The first great difference was that Charles was not a Hungarian, but ruler of a vast domain of which Hungary was only a part. The second lay in the altered numerical relationship between the 'nation' and the population of Hungary as a whole. The nation of the steppes could reasonably afford not to count its slaves and to designate itself 'the universal community of Hungarians'. Even that of St. Stephen's day must have constituted a very substantial fraction of the total population of the Hungary of the day. But the mortality through war of the families of the original freemen must have been high. Many others forfeited their status through rebellion, or without process of law, through simple inability to hold their own against a grasping and powerful neighbour. It is true that the sheer necessity of keeping in being sufficient fighting manpower to defend the country soon made the conditions of acquisition of new nobility very lax, for it was not until the fifteenth century that anyone was required to take part in this service without the reward, and then the practice was exceptional. There were eras in which any man, or any community (for bloc ennoblement was common) likely to be more useful as soldiers than taxpayers, stood more than a fair chance of ennoblement. But this recruitment barely kept pace with the wastage, and if the total number of nobles increased at all, the increase was in no proportion to that brought to the non-noble population by natural growth and immigration, forced or voluntary.

By the eighteenth century the nobles numbered only about one-twentieth of the total population. This figure was, of course, still exceedingly high compared with that of the 'nobility' in other countries, in which the title had a different meaning and the class a different origin; and that it was still so large bore striking testimony to the tenacity with which the 'nation' had clung to its birthright. But the 'nation' had now become no more than a technical, archaic term for what should really have been called a political class. It had even lost its ethnic basis of conquering race superimposed on subjects of another stock, for not only had a large part of the non-noble population become Magyarized, but the great majority of the nobles were now of non-Magyar ethnic origin. It may, however, be said at once that the latter fact proved quite irrelevant. The newcomers to the nobility, with singular uniformity, adopted the social and political outlook, and even the language, of the older members, and when the crown came to represent a foreign cause, defended against it the national cause with passion and solidarity. The change in the ethnic composition of the non-nobles became, in this connection, a source of strength to the nobles, whose national interests (to use the adjective in its modern connotation) were identical with theirs, and even the influx of non-Magyars into Hungary which took place in the eighteenth century did not alter this in practice, for national feeling was dormant among these masses until the end of the century.

Yet, diminished as its relative numbers were, the nation now exercised a far more direct and complete control over the bulk of the non-noble population than its ancestors had in St. Stephen's day. The rich, slave-owning class among its members had then probably been small enough. The lands reserved by Stephen for the crown had been extensive, and the population living on them, as direct subjects of the crown, had probably far outnumbered the nobles' slaves.

But nobility was, in theory regularly and in practice usually, linked with the ownership of noble land. If some village or group of good fighters was ennobled, nothing more might be done than declare its existing land noble; a grant of nobility to a more important figure carried with it the donation of a new estate, which might be very extensive. For centuries monarchs in distress had bought or rewarded adherents with such grants, where possible confiscated from opponents, but often, necessarily, out of their own estates, and in time, even when the property had reverted to the crown through the peaceful extinction of a family, it had become the normal practice for the crown to donate this, rather than keep it in its own hands. Thus the crown lands had dwindled away until little was left of them except those held by the Royal Free Borough sand certain privileged communities possessing charters which guaranteed them against subjection to noble rule. With the lands, the population inhabiting them passed under the control of the noble owners, whom the law entitled to exact of them, if they were socage peasants, dues and corvées which in the sixteenth and seventeenth centuries had become very heavy, while the status of the non-socage peasants was still harder.

With the exception, then, of two relatively small classes, the entire population of Hungary was composed either of noble landlords, who dominated their villeins politically and economically, or of the said villeins under noble domination. A consequence of this development was that the landowning nobles had taken the government of the local subdivisions, or counties, into their own hands. A royal official resided in each county as the king's representative; but since the later Middle Ages the affairs of the county had been managed by the local nobles, through officials elected by themselves and from among their own numbers, and responsible to Diets again composed of the local nobles. The counties could not act in contravention to the law of the land, but were autonomous.

One of the two exceptions consisted of the populations of the exempted districts, notably the mining areas and the Royal Free Boroughs, whose existence formed the chief gap in the nobles' economic control of Hungary. They owned the land, but the mines and the produce were the king's; here the nobles had no control. And the Royal Free Boroughs, inhabited for the most part by German settlers and protected by charters which often enabled them to deny nobles even the right to settle on their territory, were the chief centres of the nation's trade and industry. Hampered by the competition of the boroughs in such endeavours as they made to develop similar activities on their own lands, the nobles concentrated their efforts on weakening the position of their rivals, to the general detriment.

The other class not standing, in one capacity or the other, in the relationship described above was that known technically as the armilistae, or colloquially, as 'sandalled' (bocskoros) or 'seven-plum-tree' nobles, i.e. persons technically noble but owning only a single hide of land, or entirely landless. This class formed, numerically, a considerable proportion of the entire nobility; a census taken in 1754-5 gave 14,000 out of the 32,000 noble families registered as belonging to it. It had salvaged from the centuries little more than its personal liberties and the active suffrage in the County elections, but was not admitted to the County Diets or to the offices which exercised the real political power.

The 15,000 or so 'landed' families which possessed full

political rights constituted the real 'nation' of the eighteenth century, the true inheritors of the eleventh century. But even they had lost one of the most jealously-guarded principles of their ancestors, the complete equality of all nobles. They now fell into two categories, distinguished *de facto* and also *de jure*.

Naturally, just as some members of the old community had sunk below the common level, others had soon risen above it, and from a very early date in Hungarian history we find great families collecting into their hands vast estates which enabled them to establish, lawfully or unlawfully, a sort of semi-feudal relationship even over the lesser nobles of the locality and one of semi-independence towards the king. The national kings and the lesser nobles had the same interest in combating these oligarchies. The families fell almost as fast as they rose, and by the end of the Middle Ages the principle of constitutional equality between all nobles had been modified only in this, that the nobles had begun to send only representatives to the consultative organs on which the 'magnates' sat in person; the quality of 'magnate' was, however, still only official and not hereditary, and no office was out of reach of any noble.

Some of the kings of foreign stock had preferred to combat rebellious oligarchs, not with the help of the common nobility, but with that of another oligarchy attached to themselves. The Habsburgs, to whom the common nobility represented a foreign and rebellious element, carried on this process. They divided the Diet definitively into two Houses, in one of which the magnates appeared in person, while the other was composed of delegates, two from each County, of the common nobles, and augmented the ranks of magnates *ex officio* by conferring hereditary magnate rank, sometimes further distinguished by the hereditary title of count or baron, on certain families. In 1697 Leopold I allowed this class to depart from the Hungarian practice of dividing the family estate among all children and to found *fidei-commissa*, i.e. estates inalienably entailed in primogeniture.

This process, the whole purpose of which was to create in

Hungary a vice-royal class attached to the dynasty, reached its climax in the period preceding the Peace of Szatmár. Some of the magnates had, indeed, taken the Habsburg side, but by no means all, and in 1690 Leopold established a so-called 'Neo-acquistica Commissio', the function of which was to confiscate the lands of all Hungarian nobles whose conduct had offered any pretext whatsoever and to bestow them on reliable adherents. While some of the recipients were loyalist (labanc) Hungarians, the majority were now foreigners – generals in the Imperial armies or other servants of the Court – who were rewarded with estates in Hungary, often in lieu of arrears of pay. Up to 1715 over 250 foreign families had been so established in Hungary and the intention had been to carry on the process until all Hungary was brought, as Bohemia had been brought a century earlier, wholly under the rule of an aristocracy entirely devoted to the Habsburgs and their interests.

When all this has been written, no detailed description is needed of the settlement which was reached after Szatmár. The representative of the crown was Charles III (as Emperor Charles VI) and his only wishes were to secure peace in his rear and the succession of his own dominions, undiminished, to his daughter. In return for the Hungarians' acceptance of these wishes, with the rider that Hungary was now united *indivisibiliter et inseparabiliter* with the Austrian provinces, with the mutual obligation of defence *contra vim externam* and their consequent important further consent to the establishment of a standing army to which they would contribute, but which remained a central service, Charles simply accepted their equally simple demand, and swore to respect and preserve all the freedoms, privileges, statutes, rights and customs of Hungary and to introduce no modifications of them, except in agreement with the Diet. As the Diet was noble and nine-tenths of the said laws, privileges, etc., were those defining the position of the nobles vis-à-vis the crown and, by implication, the non-noble population, this simply meant that the nobles were now confirmed *de jure* in the position described above. The constitutional history of the rest of the century can for our purposes be summed up in a few words: Maria Theresa, when she succeeded her father, confirmed the undertakings which he had given. Her son, Joseph II, was unwilling to do so and introduced, by unilateral action, a number of drastic innovations, which, had he been able to make them lasting, would have altered the whole structure of Hungarian society; but the resistance put up by the 'nation', which did not admit the legality of these measures, was so vigorous that Joseph was forced on his deathbed to repeal the greater part of them, and his brother and successor, Leopold II, restored the *status quo*.

Various questions of interpretation had arisen during the century, and the 'nation' had yielded a minor point here and there, but wherever it saw fundamentals involved, it had stood its ground with all its traditional tenacity. It had even achieved the remarkable feat of laying entirely on the shoulders of the socage peasants the war tax to cover the upkeep of the standing army, although that institution was in practice relieving the nobles themselves of their obligation to perform that military service the performance of which justified their exemption from taxation.

What the century did bring new was a further differentiation, due to the altered economic, social and political conditions, between the various strata of the nobility itself. With the practical abolition of the noble *levée en masse* the sandalled nobles lost their *raison d'être*. The crown, which was anxious to limit the exemptions from its authority as narrowly as possible, and the wealthier nobles, who no longer felt the need of their alliance, combined against them. They lost their full immunity from taxation and almost all their political rights except that of active suffrage to the County Diets. Their memory survives as that of an unruly mob selling its votes every three years in exchange for a week's feasting. The dinners were enough; they did not even bargain for consideration of their interests.

For practical purposes the nobility now consisted of the

magnates on the one hand, and on the other, the 'bene posses-
sionati' landed nobles, later known as the 'gentry'. The magnates numbered only two or three hundred families or representatives of institutions; the gentry, some 25,000 families.
In all other respects, however, the post-Szatmár settlement had
left the two classes nicely balanced. The two Houses were
equal in authority. A few great offices were always held by
magnates, a larger number of the lesser ones by gentry. The
magnates dominated the central organs of government and
the gentry the Counties. When the great reallocation of land
ended, it left about half the noble land in the possession of
each class.

Socially and economically there were enormous differences
between the positions of the two classes. It was the magnates'
heyday. Never before had a Hungarian oligarchy enjoyed such
opportunities, not so much (after the redistribution had ended)
of acquiring wealth, but of keeping it. For the court still saw
in this class the surest support of its own rule and gave its
members every possible facility and privilege; helped them to
acquire land, protected them against losing it. Many instances
are on record of the court's paying off the debts of this or that
magnate – even, on one occasion, of the class *en bloc*.

A *latifundium* – the consolidated and centralized demesne of
a magnate – was probably at least 20,000 acres in extent and
could well extend to 50,000 or more. A single family might
possess many such units: thus the Eszterházy family, the greatest
of them all, owned at one time nearly seven million Hungarian
acres. Several other families owned estates which topped the
100,000 mark.

A large proportion of these estates lay in areas recovered
from the Turks and unburdened with servitudes. Their owners
could treat them as 'dominical' land, exempt from any obligation to the state whatever. Their production costs were thus
extremely low, low enough to enable them to make capital
investments which sometimes repaid themselves tenfold.
Money flowed into the big landowners' coffers during the

period when Austria was fighting wars on non-Hungarian soil. Many of them flourished exceedingly—built themselves grandiose castles in the neo-baroque style of the age, filled their rooms with knick-knacks from Paris and Vienna, surrounded themselves with liveried servants and obsequious hangers-on, and in general lived existences which aped as closely as possible those of sovereign princes. Prince Eszterházy's court and his great palace (which was only one of the family's many seats) at Eszterháza were, in fact, such as many a German princeling might have envied; the Grassalkovitch palace at Gödöllö did not look unworthy of its position when, later, it became the Habsburg residence.

Besides his country seat, the magnate probably owned a palace in Pozsony for sessions of the Diet, and very likely a grand town house in Vienna, where he spent part of the year attending the Imperial Court.

Very different from this was the life of the country squire, spent between his old-fashioned, one-storied, whitewashed 'curia' at the end of the village street and the equally unpretentious premises in the county town, a few miles away, where he met his neighbours and cousins to run the local affairs. It was a life not without material comfort, of a kind, because Hungary in these years 'choked in her own fat'; unable to export more than a fraction of her own produce, she ate and drank it. But it was a life of narrow horizons, limited interests, few intellectual distractions and, incidentally, still conducted largely on a pre-monetary basis. Owners of quite substantial estates found the expense of a short stay in Buda or Pozsony a heavy burden on their annual budget.

Foreign travel books usually concentrated on the magnates' palaces, so that the world came to regard the magnate as the typical Hungarian. Hungarians themselves saw the matter differently. To them the magnates were a denationalized or anti-national class, creatures of the Habsburgs and instruments of their rule. It was the gentry who preserved the old values in their own lives, fathered their peasants in the old way, safeguarded the national liberties in the County Diets against the incessant war of attrition waged against them by the centralist authorities, and thus ultimately preserved Hungary herself, her spirit and her very national identity, from extinction. There is a measure of truth in this. The gentry indeed lived close to the soil among the people, under conditions not very different from those of a prosperous peasant. They were the Magyars of the Magyars. They spoke the old language, wore the old dress, knew the *Tripartitum* (Wérböczi's codification of Hungarian law) by heart, and did time and again thwart some demand of the crown officials, passed to the Counties for action, by the simple process of declaring it illegal and refusing to execute it; in which case the crown possessed no practical means, short of violence, of enforcing its wishes.

The magnates in fact led a different life. Their leading members spent much of their time in Vienna, intermarried with the Austrian nobility, spoke French, German or Italian among themselves and often did not even know Hungarian, and in politics represented the aulic party which was loyal to the monarch and approved the implications of the Pragmatic Sanction. Yet the contrast between their political attitude, as a class, and that of the gentry should not be over-emphasized. It is a very important fact in Hungarian history that the negotiator on the Imperial side of the Peace of Szatmár, Jozsef Pálffy, had himself been a Hungarian. The Peace had saved a great deal for Hungary. Even though the examination and rejection of title-deeds went on for many years after it, the naked confiscations had stopped, and with them the hope of turning Hungary into a second Bohemia. The foreign tide even receded, for the reason that the German, Spanish or Italian generals and courtiers found that they could simply do nothing with a square league of sandy soil in the trackless middle of nowhere, inhabited, if at all, by outlandish-garbed and truculent-faced peasants whose language they could not understand. They sold their estates back to the first bidder, either a Serbian or Armenian speculator (who, if he did not sell them on, himself became a Magyar indistinguishable from the rest) or to a Hungarian. By the middle of the century the Hungarian magnate class had again become overwhelmingly Magyar. Socially they were a new class, but ancestrally of the same stock as the gentry or, in many cases for that matter, of the peasantry. Foreign names occur in their lists – Harruckers, Aspremonts and a few others – but in a minute minority beside the Eszterházys, Pálffys, Erdödys, Apponyis, Károlyis, Sigrays, etc.

And even if this class was partially denationalized, the process seldom went far. The mere fact that the Emperor's Austrian servants, and in particular the highest military circles, regarded everything Hungarian with suspicion, kept them from complete assimilation into the supra-national circle whose ideal was simply the Imperial *Gesamtmonarchie*. Few Hungarians played any important rôle in the affairs of the *Gesamtmonarchie* during the century. And it does the magnates an injustice to represent them as deliberately sacrificing Hungarian independence to that ideal – if only because it was the continued existence of the Hungarian constitution which left them in the enviable position, which the Austrian nobles had been obliged to renounce, of paying no taxes. When Joseph II tried to bring Hungary under a centralized, Germanizing bureaucracy, the magnates joined hands with the gentry in resisting him.

In their attitude towards the non-noble population of Hungary – whether peasants or burghers – the magnates were neither worse nor better than the gentry. The history of the century (unlike that of its successor) contains no case in which either class genuinely pressed social reform against the resistance of the other. And if the magnates did spend an appreciable proportion of their fortunes outside Hungary, or import foreign luxuries, they were also the only class in Hungary sufficiently in touch with the outer world to appreciate new economic ideas and new developments and with sufficient capital to carry them through. Such economic modernization as was carried through in Hungary during the century was the work of the enlightened element among the magnates, some of whom reclaimed great areas from desolation, settled flourishing villages on them, introduced modern methods of agriculture, and even founded industrial enterprises and organized the large-scale export of their produce; while the squire, unable to afford modernization even if he had understood its value, and dependent on the cheap but also wasteful socage labour, could do no more than live on among his peasants, his only economic ambition to get for himself the maximum share of the fruits of their labour. Even the cultural and national revival which, after a long period of stagnation, set in towards the close of the century, owed as much to the magnates as to the gentry. However faithfully the gentry had kept the national spirit from extinction, without new contacts and new inspiration it must yet have exhausted itself in barren reminiscence of the past. The magnates, some of whom were extraordinarily lavish in their benefactions to school and church, provided the possibility for that synthesis between new and old on which the Reform Era of the nineteenth century tried to build a new Hungary.

Magnates and gentry must after all share in fairly even measure such praise and such blame as history will allot to the Hungarian nobles of the eighteenth century. The balance sheet has, indeed, large entries on both sides. Later writers usually stressed the debits. The nobles' tenacious defence of their privileges undoubtedly prevented the evolution of Hungary into a modern state. It preserved the narrow and inequitable system of political oligarchy, and equally the unjust incidence of taxation: completely unjust now that they no longer served the state with their arms. In connection with this, the nobles throughout the century stubbornly resisted all attempts made by the crown to lighten the peasants' socage obligations. They habitually maintained that the relationship between lord and peasant was a private one with which the crown was not concerned: on one occasion the House of Magnates burst into 'uproarious laughter' when a speaker suggested that the peasants' dues should even be legally limited, and many of them were not satisfied even with the large dues and corvées then customary. It is true that the position was not quite so simple as is often supposed: the frightful depopulation after the Turkish wars had created a shortage of labour which undermined the whole structure of the landowning system, and the insistence placed by those landowners who still possessed socage cultivators on the restriction of their freedom of movement was partly a counter to the attempts made by the recipients of new estates to entice away from them the labour without which they could not live, while the crown's real purpose in pressing for reduction of the corvées was not simply to benefit the peasants, as a matter of philanthropy, but to make more of their produce and their manpower available for its own objects, i.e. for the realization of dynastic ambitions. On some occasions we find the crown demanding increased taxation and the nobles invoking the peasants' interest to refuse it. In the main, however, they were at least as selfish as any other employing class, and their refusal to accept taxation had the further consequence that the crown in retaliation refused its assistance in developing Hungary economically, applied discriminatory tariffs against it and deliberately kept it a 'colonial market' for Austrian industrial products.

On the other hand, the Hungarian nobles' constitutional liberties may have been antiquated, may have benefited only a fraction of the population of Hungary, yet they did set a limit on the despotic power of the crown. The Hungarian nobility was at the time the only class within the Habsburg Monarchy, almost the only class on the Continent, which succeeded in setting such a limit and thus maintained a position which later proved of powerful service in helping not only Hungary, but other countries also, to drive despotism into retreat at a time when despotism was no longer benevolent but only obscurantist.

Incidentally, since the ultimate aims of the authorities in Vienna were not only absolutism, but also centralization and

Germanization, the nobles, in defending their own constitution, were at the same time defending Hungary's language and her very national identity. For good or for ill, Hungary owed it to her nobles, and to them alone, that she did not become a German province in the German Reich.

8

SWEDEN

Michael Roberts

With the death of Charles XII in the trenches before Fredriks-
hald, Sweden entered abruptly upon a new phase in her
history. The 'Age of Greatness' gave place to the 'Age of
Liberty': 'the hand of Sweden's clock' (in the words of the
famous epigram) 'moved from XII to I'. The change was
a real revolution; and it was a revolution carried through
mainly by the aristocracy.

The events of 1718-20 represent the culmination of a tradition and the victory of a political principle: the tradition of
aristocratic opposition to the monarchy, the principle of limited
rather than absolute kingship. Since the Middle Ages the
nobility had been the guardians of the nation's liberties.
They had been early converts to the contractualist and mon-
archomachist theories of the later sixteenth century; and there
had even been occasions when they had evinced some hanker-
ings after *aurea libertas* on the Polish pattern. Erik Sparre's
programme of 1594, the Charter extorted from Gustavus
Adolphus in 1612, the Form of Government of 1634, the
Additament of 1660 were all stages in one protracted constitutional debate. In 1680 Charles XI had seized a favourable
opportunity to reassert the rival theory of popular absolutism,
and for a generation thereafter constitutionalism had been
driven underground. Charles XI and Charles XII had been
'sovereign', and it was against 'sovereignty' in all its implications that the nobility reacted in 1719 and 1720. The
Estates – especially after 1729 – did, no doubt, come to assume

to themselves very extensive powers; but even their warmest apologists shrank from terming them 'sovereign': their official designation was simply 'power-owning' (*maktägande*). On paper, indeed, the Constitution of 1720 continued to reserve, in phraseology now somewhat antique, a specific·share in the government to King and Senate; but in fact, as the Age of Liberty settled into its stride, the Estates drew most of the functions of government into the hands of their committees; the king's veto was neutralized by the name-stamp; and the enforcement of ministerial responsibility by the repeated use of something akin to impeachment (*licentiering*) reduced the Senate at last to a condition of tremulous subjection.

In this growing absolutism the Estate of Nobility had the greatest share. Theoretically, no doubt, each of the four Estates had an equal portion of power: in reality, the weight of the first Estate was for long decisive. The danger of a clash between the nobility and the lower Estates, which had been serious for some years after 1718, diminished after 1723; and from the late 'thirties to the mid-'sixties the Estate of Burghers, from which the strongest challenge to the nobility might have been expected, was bound to it by close party ties, since each was usually strongly Hat. The first Estate enjoyed double representation on all those highly developed committees where the real business of the Diet was transacted; its members filled a majority of the more important positions in the king's service; and its Speaker, the Marshal of the Diet, by his position as permanent chairman of the Secret Committee, could do so much to determine the course of parliamentary business that his influence was said to be worth fifty votes. The Nobility even claimed a *votum decisivum*, which would have been tantamount to a veto upon the resolutions of the other Estates; and though it never made this claim good, it could and did block the decisions of the Diet by objecting that they trenched upon its privileges. It is true that the Swedish electoral system was such that as a rule the members of the nobility had little or no influence upon elections for the other Estates: Sweden had no

borough patrons. And it is true, too, that the division into
Estates precluded the younger son of a nobleman from sitting
among the burghers or peasants, and that it was extremely
rare for the nobility to enter the Church. But even without
these aids the Swedish aristocracy was probably in a stronger
political position than the English peerage.

The *Riddarhus*, where the Nobility held its debates, was
indeed the real centre of Swedish political life. The first
Estate, by its size (it was more than three times as big as all the
others put together), its political talent and its constitutional
traditions, was the real leader of the nation. The milling crowds
of nobles that came up to the Diet (on a critical division the
numbers in the *Riddarhus* might exceed a thousand) made party
organization a necessity: it was among the nobility that the
first party bosses emerged, with their 'operators', their caucus
voting and their political clubs. It was in the *Riddarhus* that
the notorious corruption of political life was concentrated. It
was not that the nobility as a class was less patriotic than the
rest of the nation, or more willing to sell itself to a foreign
power; the influence of foreign gold upon political behaviour
has in any case probably been exaggerated, and it seems likely
that many members of the Diet took bribes only for voting
according to their own convictions, and chose their paymasters
to square with their consciences. But because the Nobility was
the most important Estate, it drew to it the greatest share of the
foreign ministers' attentions. The election of a Marshal, the
securing of suitable benchmen, the gaining a majority among
the noble members of the Secret Committee – these were the
great objects for which France and Russia and England spent
their money so lavishly. Most of British secret service expenditure in Sweden went upon buying the proxies of peers, or
upon paying the travelling expenses and maintenance allowances of impecunious noblemen. Just how poor some of them
were, and how cheaply they were prepared to sell their votes
upon occasion, may be seen from Sir John Goodricke's estimates for 1765, when no less than two hundred of them were

to be paid subsistence allowances at the very modest rate of £3 10s. a month.

The nobility in the eighteenth century was a numerous class: in 1718 it may have numbered some ten thousand members, or something over a thousand families, in a population of one and a half million (or one and three-quarters, if we include Finland). But it was far from being a unified or homogeneous body. It showed marked differences in geographical distribution, paternal origin, material wealth and type of occupation. Geographically, it lay thickest in the Mälar region, in Skåne, and around Jönköping: in Dalarna, and over the whole of Norrland, it was represented only by a handful of resident officials. Between the titled nobility – the counts and barons – and the mass of hungry officers who constituted the majority of the Estate lay a perceptible gulf, and at times a very real antagonism, especially in the period of Arvid Horn's ministry. In 1719 the high aristocracy had tried to entrench their pre-eminence; but the abolition in that year of the division of the nobility into three classes had been the first sign that the 'Riddarhus-democracy' (as it was termed) was resentful of the political pretensions of the magnates; the alteration in 1734 of the method of electing benchmen (whereby procedure by ballot and lot was substituted for open voting) in effect emancipated the lesser nobles from the political influence of the greater; and the fall of Horn in 1738 signified among other things the triumph of 'democracy' over 'aristocracy' within the first Estate. Thereafter the title of count or baron counted for less and less: for the next thirty years it was the lesser nobility that really ruled Sweden.

To some extent the distinction between higher and lower nobility coincided with the distinction (equally important in the politics of the day) between the old landed families and the new nobility of service. Though it is true that there were men of ancient lineage who lived modestly as simple country squires, and though it is no less true that the tradition of state service was deeply implanted in the oldest and wealthiest noble houses, yet on the whole it may be said that the historic families – those Oxenstiernas, Bielkes, Brahes, Posses, Bondes, Sparres, Horns, who in the high summer of Sweden's glory had enjoyed almost a prescriptive right to membership of the Senate – were families whose wealth and consequence came from landed possessions rather than from the emoluments of office. This remained true even after Charles XI's *reduktion* had fallen with capricious severity upon very many of them. But side by side with them there had grown up a new nobility: men who had made a career for themselves in the civil service or the armed forces, and who owed their ennoblement to merits acquired and rank attained in the king's employ. No doubt they very soon became landed proprietors themselves; but in the eyes of the old senatorial families they remained *novi homines*: when Samuel Åkerhielm was made Master of Ceremonies to Frederick I, the appointment provoked a contemptuous snort from Countess Sigrid Bonde. And behind these more eminent *arrivistes* lay troops of nobles in middling or poor circumstances, who 'won their meagre bread' (as they put it) in the service of the crown. For, on the whole, the Swedish aristocracy was a working aristocracy, an aristocracy of bureaucrats, soldiers and sailors; and for many of them their comfort, and even their livelihood, depended upon a good job and fair promotion. Of this bureaucratic aristocracy Charles XI had been the real chief. But Charles XII, in the stress of his closing years, had attempted to override and break through the bureaucratic hierarchy which his father had bequeathed to him: and though he fell before the attempt had made much headway, it gave to the changes of 1718-20 much of their character. The revolution of those years was not only the reaction of a Whiggish aristocracy against absolutism: it was also the reaction of a partly noble bureaucracy against arbitrary interference with the bureaucratic machine.

The number of nobles holding positions in the public service was, both absolutely and relatively, very considerable. In the civil service it varied between about 200 and 300; in the armed forces between about 900 and 1300. These figures indicate that anything from two-fifths (in 1730) to one-half (in 1720 and again in 1790) of the adult male nobility served the king. In the army, the noble officers accounted for between one-third (in 1719) and almost three-quarters (in 1757) of the whole establishment. In the central offices of government the percentage of nobles was anything from about 85 per cent (in 1720) to about 42 per cent (in 1792). In local government they had a monopoly of the office of lord-lieutenant (*landshövding*), and supplied from one-fifth to two-fifths of the sheriffs (*häradshövdingar*); while most of the provincial judges (*lagmän*) were drawn from their ranks. In general, the percentage of nobles tended to fall throughout the period, in all branches; but it did not fall steadily, and even in 1792 the aristocracy was overwhelmingly preponderant in the highest positions. These facts explain the passionate interest, all through the Age of Liberty, in questions concerning appointments and promotions. The great parliamentary crises tended to group themselves round such questions; the inquisitions into the conduct of ministers, undertaken upon an alteration of the party majority in the Diet, paid particular attention to them; and in the years just before 1772 they provided one of the main bones of contention between the Nobility and the lower Estates. But the control of appointments had not only a personal interest for most members of the *Riddarhus*; it had an obvious constitutional aspect too: if the right to appoint were left in the hands of the king, he might gain control of the Diet, since in all Estates save that of the Peasants, and most especially in the Nobility, a considerable proportion of the members were office-holders. It was a quarrel on just this point that led to the introduction of the name-stamp in 1756. The 'Report on the Services' (*Tjänstebetänkande*) of the same year was an attempt to lay down permanent rules for promotion, independently of royal favour, and on a basis of strict seniority. The craving for office among the aristocracy was indeed such that many nobles are said to have sold their land in order to buy an office with the proceeds;

many were prepared to accept government posts even though no salary might be attached to them (for the emoluments of an office were often allocated by way of pension to the retiring incumbent); and there grew up in the civil service a trade in offices analogous to the sale of commissions in the army. Moreover, since a state of war brought with it an expansion of the military and naval establishments, and hence brighter prospects of a livelihood for the needier members of the nobility, war (or at least the prospect of war) tended to be popular with such people; and this provides an additional explanation for the bellicosity of the earlier Hats – the party above all of the *Riddarhus*-democracy.

The economic position of many of the nobility thus depended upon salaries and wages: as one of them remarked in 1719, the aristocracy must support itself '*litteris aut armis*'. But the rewards of service were not very brilliant, even when they were punctually paid; and the economic strength of the aristocracy came mainly from other sources, and not least from land. Large-scale agriculture for the market was increasing, especially in Skåne and the Mälar region; but for many nobles the bulk of their income from the land came in rents and labour-services. Noble land was relieved of many burdens, and it could be worked very cheaply, since most of the labour was provided by the obligatory day-work of the tenants on the estate, and noble landlords (especially in the old Danish provinces of the south) had few scruples about making very heavy exactions in this regard; while as to the rest of the labourers, their wages were artificially depressed by legislation (notably in 1723 and 1739) designed to ensure an abundant supply of hands. It was only in the second half of the century that the policy of using mainly wage-labourers began to be recognized (largely upon noble initiative) as an agronomically preferable alternative. But in many parts of Sweden land was valuable, not so much for the crops it could produce, or the stock it could support, as for the mineral riches that lay beneath it; and one major source of the wealth of the aristocracy lay in the mining, or the manufacture, of iron. A fair proportion of the leading ironmasters of the eighteenth century were men of noble birth, and perhaps as many had been elevated to the peerage. The ennoblement of great industrialists brought fresh capital into the aristocracy, and enabled it to play a considerable part in financing further industrial enterprises and new mercantile ventures. There were many noble shareholders, for instance, in the Falun copper-mine; the manufactures – at Alingsås, Rörstrand, Vedevåg – upon which the Hats lavished such excessive concessions, had usually plenty of nobles among their directors; and noble ironmasters could find money for investment in new equipment and better processes. Even the East India Company, though established – like most trading ventures – by foreign capital, soon came to be dominated by native directors, many of whom belonged to the aristocracy. The merchant houses of Stockholm were able to raise loans from the industrialists among the nobility, though oftener (as with Grill and K. G. Tessin) it was the merchant who helped the spendthrift noble out of his difficulties. But the free capital of the aristocracy came from the mines and the forges, rather than from agriculture; or it came from marriage into the families of moneyed men (which was of fairly frequent occurrence); or, finally, from the financiers and merchants themselves, who entered the ranks of the peerage, abandoned commerce, and went into iron-manufacturing.

Peerages of this type reflect the fact that the Swedish aristocracy in this century was anything but a closed caste. It was, on the contrary, constantly receiving quite large accessions of fresh blood. The Constitution of 1720 had severely restricted the king's right to create peers; but the limitation was frequently ignored in the course of the next half-century, usually with the connivance of the Estates, or even upon their suggestion. Between 1719 and 1792 some 624 families (or 725 individuals) were ennobled; and though this increase was nearly balanced by the number of peerages that became extinct, it at least assured a perennial rejuvenescence. But it placed an intolerable strain upon the limited seating accommodation of the *Riddarhus*. The nobility steadily resisted all suggestions that they should elect a reasonable number of persons to represent the whole Estate, for they feared electoral corruption of the English type, and gloried in being their own constituents. The consequent crowding of the *Riddarhus* certainly contributed to the tumultuous and unseemly character sometimes assumed by the debates of that assembly. It was partly in order to meet this inconvenience that the nobility in 1762 took a unanimous resolution not to permit the introduction of any new peers until the membership of the House had fallen to 800. The resolution did not debar new creations: it meant only that for a long time to come no new peers would be able to take their seats. Peer-creating therefore continued, though Gustavus III in 1772 promised not to add more than 150 to the existing number.

The new peers were recruited, as to the great majority of them, from reputable sources: it was only rarely that the *Riddarhus* was asked to accept such creations as that of Daniel Schedvin, a simple corporal who was ennobled in 1756 as a reward for betraying Erik Brahe's plot. Much the largest number of peerages went to the army and navy, and to the civil service (as far as possible, in equal proportions): in each of them ennoblement was thought of almost as the necessary consequence of the attainment of a certain grade. But the aristocracy was also supplied from other sources than these. It became usual to ennoble the children of bishops, even in their father's lifetime – a practice which gave some concern to the Estate of Clergy, as compromising their professional solidarity. It was not uncommon, as we have seen, to ennoble business-men, industrialists and entrepreneurs. And there was an admirable readiness to ennoble persons of distinction in the world of learning, science, literature or art: such names as Linnaeus, Olof Dalin, Polhem, Scheele, Lagerbring, Swedenborg, Nordencrantz, Hårleman are typical of a quite large class. Compared even with the English peerage, the Swedish nobility must seem extraordinarily diverse in origin, various in talent and, in the true sense, aristocratic. It was as though Pope and Priestley, James Watt and Gibbon, Adam Smith and Nicholas Hawksmoor had all sat on the same benches with Lord Carrington, Lord Rodney and the first Lord Liverpool.

In Sweden the quality of nobility extended to all the children of a noble, and to all his descendants in the male line. Each noble family sent one representative to the Diet – normally, though not necessarily, its *caput*. Attendance at the Diet was no longer compulsory, and hence it happened that *capita* could entrust their proxies to political allies, or sell them to the highest bidder. Families which had been ennobled, or naturalized, but which had not been introduced into the *Riddarhus*, remained unrepresented there, though in all other respects they shared in the privileges of their order. These privileges were of ancient origin, and were to be considered as the reward for military service rendered in time of war; but that aspect of the question had by this time been almost forgotten. The most important of them was exemption, total or partial, from those basic taxes which formed the ordinary revenues of the crown. The manor (*sätesgård*) inhabited and farmed by its owner was totally exempt: other noble lands paid as a rule at half-rates. On a manor, the tenants rendered to their lord all those dues and services which (if they had been crown tenants or freeholders) they would have rendered to the crown; on non-manorial lands they rendered half to the landlord and half to the crown. The amount of noble land had been considerably diminished by Charles XI's *reduktion*, and it was now forbidden to increase it; hence, as new families entered the peerage, the competition for noble land, with all the economic advantages it entailed, became keener. The situation was exacerbated by the increasing passage of such land into non-noble hands: an estate might be pawned to a creditor and never redeemed, or an heiress might marry a commoner. From 1719 to 1723 the nobility strove to halt this process by extorting from the monarchy privileges which visited *mésalliance* with severe penalties, and which prohibited the ownership of noble land by commoners. The attempt was a failure. The privileges of 1723 represented a retreat from the extreme claims of 1719: thereafter only peasants were to be debarred from acquiring noble lands; the nobleman's right of pre-emption on any land offered for sale within his family was much curtailed; and the penalties for marriage with a commoner were greatly softened. By collusive actions, special exemptions and simple violation of the law, the transfer of noble land into non-noble hands went briskly on; and though nobles usually managed to prevent commoners from getting hold of manors, there was little to hinder other noble lands from changing hands. And as the aristocracy lost its monopoly of noble land, it found itself more and more forced to buy land which was not noble, since noble land was not to be had. This was particularly true in Skåne and the Mälar provinces, where agriculture for a market encouraged landlords to build up large and unified estates. By 1772 the distinction between noble and non-noble land was already beginning to break down: it has been calculated that whereas in 1718 some 6·7 per cent of noble land was in the possession of commoners, in 1772 the figure had risen to 16·3 per cent. As to marriage outside the nobility, it seems that at the beginning of the period – thanks mainly to an excess of females which was a consequence of the losses of the nobility in Charles XII's wars – about one-third of all the marriages contracted by the aristocracy were with commoners, while at the end of it the proportion was between two-fifths and one-half.

Other privileges of the nobility included a *forum privilegiatum* for certain offences; the right of presentation to livings in those parishes within which their manors lay; and the monopoly (in certain provinces only) of hunting and fishing on their own lands. As to the last of these, their position was already weakening: attempts to have this privilege entrenched in the new Code of 1734 were defeated; and though hunting rights were not then formally abolished, they remained henceforward upon the uncertain legal basis of ordinance rather than of statute.

More important than any of these was the right, firmly established by the privileges of 1723, to a monopoly of the highest appointments in the service of the state. An ordinance of 1714 (suspended in 1766, but renewed in 1774) graded Swedish society into forty classes. In 1723 a line was drawn between the eleventh and twelfth classes, corresponding respectively to the army ranks of colonel and lieutenant-colonel. Henceforward offices in the eleventh class and upwards were to be reserved to the nobility: no one who was not a noble could be appointed, for instance, to the Senate, nor be made a lord-lieutenant, or an admiral, or a president of one of the Supreme Courts (*hovrätter*). As time went on, however, this limitation was a good deal modified in practice. On the one hand frequent ennoblements opened a way to the highest offices to those not of aristocratic birth; while on the other the bar imposed by the privileges of 1723 was continually weakened by exceptions. By the close of the Age of Liberty the monopoly had become very nearly a dead letter, except as to membership of the Senate; and even so high an office as that of vice-president of the Supreme Court in Stockholm was from 1758 held by a commoner. These developments explain the violent outburst of indignation on the part of the lower Estates in 1770, when the Senate excluded a highly qualified commoner from consideration for appointment as vice-president of the Supreme Court at Åbo. It was felt that the aristocracy was trying to revive a privilege already obsolescent; and the controversy about noble privileges became the central point in the bitter internal struggle which in 1772 brought Sweden's constitutional experiment in ruins to the ground.

The constitutional arrangements of 1720 had never been quite as enthusiastically received by the commonalty as by the aristocracy. The Estate of Peasants, shut out (save for a few brief periods of crisis) from the Secret Committee, and made to feel their inferiority, had long been restive. During the rising of the Dalesmen in 1743 there had been evidence of anti-aristocratic feeling, and very clear signs that the lower orders might prefer a popular absolutism on the Danish model to a liberty which advantaged only their betters. In the 'sixties some of these feelings, long suppressed, came to the surface. The great Cap victory of 1765, when the wrongs of a generation were avenged, and the misdeeds of two decades of Hat rule brought to judgment, was essentially the victory of the lower clergy, the smaller towns and the peasants over a nobility and bureaucracy rendered more unpopular than ever by a post-war economic crisis. The Estate of Nobility now found itself, for the first time for forty years, on the defensive. It was increasingly unable to sway the Diet, because it was faced by a solid front of the non-noble Estates. Its resolutions, delayed by the cumbrous procedure which was one effect of its swollen numbers, were now impotent to affect the Diet's decision, since that decision had already been arrived at by the concordant – and speedier – resolutions of the three lower Estates. The days were gone by when the Clergy or Peasants were prepared to alter their resolutions in deference to the appeals or threats or protests of the Nobility. The aristocracy's declining influence now led them to insist, more sharply than for some time past, upon their privileges; and this hardening of their attitude in turn provoked attacks upon them of unprecedented bitterness. Cutting across the party strife of Hats and Caps, there was now emerging a struggle between one Estate and the rest, a struggle of privileged against unprivileged, of 'workers against wasters' (*närande mot tärande*). Popular pamphlets against the nobility appealed to Swedish historical romanticism by idealizing the free yeoman (*odalbonden*) of primitive Scandinavia. The yeoman, it was argued, should have his privileges too; and in 1769-70 there was much discussion of a draft of such privileges, produced by one Kepplerus. The agitation, indeed, showed signs of carrying all before it: in Gustavus III's Charter of 1772 the king was forced to promise that all appointments to offices should be made upon merit; and had the Age of Liberty endured much longer, the peasants might well have made good their claim to membership of the Secret Committee, and even of the Senate. It seemed at least possible, in 1771 and 1772, that Sweden might be on the eve of some such revolution as was to occur in France twenty years later.

From this predicament the aristocracy was saved by Gustavus III's *coup d'état*. As long ago as 1742 Olof Dalin, in his so-called epic *Den svenska friheten (Swedish Liberty)*, had warned his countrymen that liberty might be lost as well by licence as by servility. The internecine conflicts of the Diet of 1771-2, coming as the climax to so many years' reckless use of power by the Estates, disgusted the nation with parliamentarism, and made men ready for a fresh start. This popular temper, combined with the lively alarms of the aristocracy, gave Gustavus the opportunity which his ambition had long been seeking; and the revolution of 1772, thanks to his skill and nerve, was carried through without resistance and without bloodshed. Yet, for all that, it was a revolution weighed down from the start by inherent contradictions. It was at once an action to save Sweden from the fate of Poland, which the king believed to be impending over her; a blow for 'legal despotism' on the model of Mercier de la Rivière; and the rescue of the aristocracy from the dangers which seemed to beset it. The two latter aspects, at least, were fundamentally irreconcilable. Under the influence of their fears, and to preserve their special privileges, the aristocracy in 1772 had renounced their traditional rôle of champions of constitutionalism. They had turned their backs on two hundred years of history, and aided the monarchy to free itself from the control of the nation. Henceforward the king was to be fettered only by the fragile chains of his own political virtue, and subject only to such restraints as he might think proper to incorporate into his self-drawn constitution. Gustavus III might profess to revive kingship in the style of Gustavus Adolphus; but from the point of view of the nobility it might too easily become a kingship in the style of Charles XI – or even of Charles IX. Once the immediate advantages of alliance with the monarchy had been secured, it was inevitable that the aristocracy should recur to its historic tradition, especially when that tradition, by a discreet eclecticism, could find reinforcement in the writings of French and American political theorists.

Gustavus III did not perceive this. All his prejudices predisposed him to favour the aristocracy, and few kings of Sweden have been more sympathetic by temperament to the pretensions of birth. It was his foible to regard himself as the first nobleman in his kingdom, and on more than one occasion he appeared in the *Riddarhus* in the capacity of *caput* of the Vasa family. In 1778 he revived the division of the nobility into three classes, and thus re-established 'aristocracy' within the first Estate. Lesser nobles were not welcomed at court; there was a project to reserve certain regiments exclusively to the higher nobility; and as late as 1785 the king was meditating the elimination of commoners from all commissioned ranks in the army. But this attitude did not extend to the admission even of the highest aristocracy to real political power: the inner ring of the king's advisers, though usually ennobled, were new men, and regarded as upstarts; and Lilliestråle's purification of the local government and the judiciary fell heavily upon noble office-holders. Gustavus, in fact, conceived the aristocracy as Louis XIV had conceived it – as a splendid decoration around the throne. If they were but willing to devote themselves to the mummery of mock orders of chivalry, to immerse themselves in the complexities of court etiquette, and to cultivate an insatiable appetite for amateur theatricals, they had done all that he could require of them.

The Swedish aristocracy soon found this rôle unsatisfying. By 1778 the first signs of a revival of constitutional opposition had appeared; by 1786 the first Estate was at loggerheads with the king; by 1788 some of them had pushed contractualist or jusnaturalist theory to its uttermost consequence. The king's breach of his own constitution was answered by the treason of Anjala. The events of 1788-9 in their turn forced Gustavus to hasten on the revolution to which he had been tending since

1786. All attempts to conciliate the aristocracy were abandoned, and the Act of Union and Security sealed the alliance of the crown with the lower Estates. In return for new constitutional concessions which made him more nearly absolute, Gustavus destroyed the essential privileges of the nobility. Non-manorial lands might henceforth be freely acquired even by peasants; the hunting rights of the aristocracy were extended to all owners of land; and the provision that almost all appointments should be made upon merit alone left little remaining of the noble monopoly of office. Before the end of the reign the Senate had virtually ceased to exist; a peasant was a member of the king's government; and Gustavus was considering the replacement of the four Estates by a bicameral legislature on British models.

It was a great social revolution, foreshadowing the end of the old system of politics, and it may well have preserved Sweden from infection by French principles. Yet it probably did no more than give legislative expression to the social situation as it existed. The nobility, who had thus been deprived of their privileged position, had already lost the leadership of which their privileges had been at once the symbol and the reward. The *coup* of 1772 had dammed back the advance of the commons for less than a decade. Soon after 1780 – long before the king was forced into courting them – the non-noble classes were flooding into the services more numerously than ever. By the end of the reign the aristocracy had lost perhaps as much as one-fifth of all the noble land. The political influence of the first Estate was gone, now that the king had tamed the Diet; its social exclusiveness (never as marked as in some other countries) was already breaking down here and there – as, for instance, at the universities, where, by the close of the period, the nobility were ceasing to keep themselves aloof from other undergraduates and were entering the Nations; and even their cultural leadership was visibly passing into other hands. Thirty or forty years before, the aristocracy had dominated Swedish intellectual life. As a class they were receptive to the great

European currents of thought, whether English or (more usually) French, and they developed on their own account an exceptionally advanced body of constitutional theory upon the basis of the Constitution of 1720. They were interested in science and its applications, for many of them had been industrialists or savants themselves. They were liberal patrons of the arts, and their country houses – even though they might be of very modest dimensions – were real centres of culture and enlightenment in the remote backwoods. In K. G. Tessin they produced the Magnus de la Gardie of the age. Tessin, by his intimate ties with Parisian society, did more than any man to implant the passion for all things French – a passion which extended to the adoption of many grotesque Gallicisms into the polite jargon of the day – and for a generation he was the real arbiter of taste. Swedish painting flourished under such patronage; Swedish musical life took shape round the *Riddarhus* concerts; Swedish oratory reached a remarkably high level in the *Riddarhus* debates. And in literature, there was hardly a major author, between 1718 and 1772, who did not bear a noble name. But after 1772 came a gradual change. The influx of learned or ingenious persons – and, not less importantly, of fresh capital – into the peerage declined: in the decade 1781-90 there were only twenty-one new creations, in the last two years of the reign only one. To Tessin's position as arbiter of taste succeeded Tessin's pupil, Gustavus III. The rising middle-class began to set its stamp upon the arts. A conscious nation-alism in culture became apparent, exemplified in Gustavus III's dramatic writings, and in his invention of the 'Swedish costume'. The aristocratic predominance in literature came to an end. Creutz and Oxenstierna, no doubt, lived on into the new age, and Oxenstierna is a good example of the king's *penchant* for the old nobility; but the great writers of the Gustavian era were mostly bourgeois: Leopold, Thorild, Kell-gren, and above all Bellman, the poet of Stockholm life, who with calculated humour employed the faded aristocratic diction of pastoral poetry to portray the lewd loves of drunken corporals and demireps, and hung a Boucher landscape as background to Hogarthian orgies. When the Swedish Academy was constituted in 1786, six of the eighteen were commoners, – which would have been almost inconceivable a generation earlier. And already, in decorous doméstic anonymity, Anna Maria Lenngren – the personification, as a sort of poetic Jane Austen, of the common sense, shrewdness and wit of the upper middle-classes – was embarking on those *Attempts at Poetry* which were later to put her in the foremost place among Sweden's women writers.

By 1792, indeed, the rôle of the Swedish aristocracy was almost played out. Economic power had already been shifting towards the 'Skeppsbro-nobility' of Stockholm, the naturalized merchants of Göteborg, and the non-noble ironmasters. The boom in Sweden's export industries in the 'eighties reinforced this trend. The social and political functions of the aristocracy were passing to those 'persons of standing' (*ståndspersoner*) – the professional men, small gentry, rural industrialists, non-noble civil servants – for whom the old division of society into Estates had been unable to find a place. The nobility still spoke the language of freedom; it still believed itself to be the bearer and custodian of a great historical tradition; and it could even profess the fashionable cult of Brutus, and produce a tyrannicide. But its concept of liberty had become narrow and sterile: political liberty for the upper classes, and a Whiggish distrust of the monarchy. Social liberty it strenuously resisted; and equality and fraternity were not among its watchwords. Its obstinate defence of privilege alienated the masses; and its treatment of its tenantry was already attracting the attention of reformers. The heirs of Erik Sparre had gone bankrupt: the future belonged to other men.

9

POLAND

A. Bruce Boswell

It is important before discussing the position of the Polish nobility in the eighteenth century to explain how the Polish State was constituted. This is due to the ignorance outside Poland of a State which only appears in our text-books at the time of its decadence and partition and of which most accounts are influenced by the disparaging views of the partitioning Powers, anxious to justify themselves before the tribunal of history. Poland originally consisted of Great Poland (capital Poznań), Little Poland (capital Cracow), Silesia (capital Wroclaw), Mazovia (later capital Warsaw) and Eastern Pomerania (capital Dantzig). In 1340 Silesia and Pomerania were lost but compensation was found in the East when Galicia (capital Lwów) was annexed. Poland also attracted into her orbit some of her neighbours and carried out a dynastic union with Lithuania, which then included most of western Russia. By the recovery of Pomerania and the conquest of Prussia, part of Livonia and Kurland and for a time suzerainty over Moldavia, the Polish-Lithuanian State became one of the largest States in Europe and remained so till the eighteenth century. Internally, Poland was a kingdom, which, like Germany and Russia, broke up for two centuries into a number of principalities held together by its ecclesiastical unity and by the relationship of its princes, many of them efficient and often brilliant rulers of the dynasty of Piast, which ruled Poland from the dawn of its history till 1370. From that time, like England, Poland was ruled mainly by kings of foreign origin. The nobility emerged under the early kings and princes in two groups. The Magnates, or *Nobiles*, formed the Prince's Council which ultimately developed into the Upper House of the Polish Parliament. From this class came the high officials in Church and State, who aided the princes in the administration of the country. Below the magnates in the social and political scale were the *milites*, who originally formed the prince's army and often received land in return for service. Both these classes, at first fluid and recruited from the mass of the people, began to acquire privileges. The decisive moment in this development was the death of the last king of the Piast dynasty in 1370, which gave the Polish magnates the opportunity to extract more important privileges from his foreign successors. In 1374 Louis, Angevin king of Hungary, gave a great charter to the Polish nobles, who extended the power thus obtained when they chose his daughter as their ruler and brought about her marriage with the Grand Prince of Lithuania, and made election the future method of filling the throne.

Thus an accidental circumstance proved a fundamental factor in the development of the nobility. A second important cause of the rapid growth of the nobility was an internal one. As the magnates began to follow western customs, in adopting first slogans or war-cries and then coats of arms, the great mass of the *milites* followed their example. At that time Poland was at an earlier stage of her social development than her western neighbours. Whereas among the latter individuals and families adopted armorial bearings, in Poland, where the clan organization had not died out, a whole clan would adopt the same coat of arms. Consequently the nobility so established was a very large body, and there grew up in Poland a numerous upper class, including not only the magnates but the great mass of what in other countries would be called gentry and yeomen. This body assumed the title of the *Szlachta* (from a German word meaning 'noble'). The lower elements in this body of nobles began to take a part in State affairs along with the magnates and to claim equality of birth with that class. The members of the new body consisted mainly of landowners, but land was not the first basis of their status, since many of them had plots no larger than those of the peasants. They consolidated their position, and by the middle of the fifteenth century were closing the entry to their class when historical events gave them a great opportunity of enhancing their position in the community. Hitherto the charters had given the nobility immunity from taxation without their own consent and a number of privileges culminating in the Polish *habeas corpus*, the famous act *Neminem captivabimus nisi iure victum*. The outbreak of the great war with the Teutonic Order forced the king to undertake military tasks beyond his resources, since the old-fashioned militia was giving place to professional mercenary soldiers. In return for grants of money the *szlachta* obtained a series of charters giving them considerable political influence in their local assemblies (*sejmiki*), in which the nobility as a whole met in each province to debate local affairs, and now began to make grants to the king when he needed more money for the campaigns in Prussia in which the majority of the nobles were reluctant to serve. To facilitate this procedure, the king found it convenient to summon, from time to time, a general assembly, the *sejm*, consisting of deputies from all the local *sejmiki*. In this way a system of representative government grew up in which the king, his council, now transformed into the Senate, and the House of Deputies formed a parliament, the *sejm*, in which the *szlachta* became the predominant element, and even the monarchy became elective in the next century. The towns, partly foreign by origin, did not exercise their original rights to representation for long. The development of Polish agriculture for export was carried out almost entirely by the *szlachta*, who were able to use the peasants as serf labour and make great profits for themselves. The loss of the great trade route through Cracow and Lwów led to the economic decline of the towns and the merchants.

The predominant position attained by the *szlachta*, the privileges of its members and the equality between all sections of its class attracted the attention of neighbouring nobilities. The Lithuanian nobles after the union were granted rights similar to those of the Poles. The same rights were extended to the Ruthenians of Galicia and Lithuania, while the gentry of Prussia, Livonia, Kurland and Moldavia were all attracted by the glamour of the Polish system as compared with the monarchical or oligarchic systems of other countries. The whole upper class of these countries tended to adopt Polish names and the Polish language even when the peasants continued to speak their native tongues. The newly established class eagerly absorbed the culture of the Humanist movement and were deeply impressed by the revolutionary ideas of the Hussites, the Lutherans and the Calvinists. The 'golden age' of Polish literature, distinguished by its poets, its satirists and its constructive political and social theorists, was a great achievement by the new class, which not only held political power in its own countries, but exported, to England for instance, corn, reformers like Laski and ambassadors able to argue with Elizabeth in Latin, while they showed Europe an example of religious toleration and of a method of ruling a great state by a large representative body without recourse to autocracy or oligarchy. The reaction of the counter-reformation changed much of this. The Jesuits came to control education, and, by inculcating religious orthodoxy rather than free learning and citizenship, destroyed that individual sense of responsibility which was essential to maintain the free institutions of the *szlachta*. Without the collaboration of a large number of educated individuals with civic and moral standards, the Polish system of government could not be carried on successfully. Decline began, and the beginning of the eighteenth century saw the lowest point reached. The middle of that century saw the First Partition, but it also saw the turn of the tide – the beginning of a great revival.

In the first half of the eighteenth century the *szlachta* were predominant in the Polish Commonwealth. The king was a foreigner, elected by the *szlachta* from among a number of candidates. The towns were in a sad state of decay and the citizens had lost the right they formerly enjoyed to participate in State affairs. The church, the law courts and even the executive were mainly in the hands of members of the *szlachta*. It had, with some exceptions, closed all entry to its ranks and continued to cling jealously to its privileges and to guard its 'golden freedom'. These privileges included exemption from taxation, dues and tariffs, freedom from military service, and complete control of the Legislature, the Judiciary and the power to paralyse the Executive. This was the ancient liberty enjoyed by the Poles in contrast to the autocratic or oligarchic interference in the affairs of the nobility of other states.

The main characteristics of the *szlachta* were: (i) that, despite geographical and racial differences, it was almost entirely Polish in speech and sentiment, though landowners in the east spoke to their peasants in Lithuanian or Russian dialects and many families in Pomerania, Prussia and Livonia bore names of German origin. Old institutions survived, such as the separate ministers for the crown, i.e. Poland, and for the Grand Principality, i.e. Lithuania; separate armies and alternate meetings of the *sejm* in Warsaw and Grodno continued. But such survivals had no practical importance.

(ii) that the great mass of the *szlachta* were members of the Roman Catholic Church. During the Reformation many had become Protestants and such Dissentients, even the Unitarians, had been tolerated. Only gradually had these groups become small minorities, and the return to the Catholic Church had been accentuated by the fact that the most important of Poland's neighbours and enemies were Protestant or Orthodox. So strong was this feeling that the Poles abandoned their old toleration of minorities, whose cause was championed by aggressive neighbours. In this century the 'Dissidents', Protestants and Orthodox, were used as pawns in the political game by Frederick II and the Empress Catherine II, neither of whom was otherwise famous for religious zeal. The accusation of intolerance was one of the main arguments used to justify the interference which culminated in the First Partition. Their rights were restored later on in the century, but the matter gave rise to the great religious and national protest against foreign interference known as the Confederation of Bar in 1768, the revival of strong sentiments which were religious as well as national.

(iii) that the *szlachta* were nearly all landed gentry. Their outlook was embodied in the phrase *bene natus et possessionatus*, and in the cruder idea that they were descendants of Japhet, the word Ham being used as a term of contempt for the serf. But the old distinction between magnates and gentry, always latent, but forgotten in the days of agricultural prosperity and social equality, had been revived in the seventeenth century, which saw the rise of vast estates in Lithuania and the Ukraine which not only overweighted the position of the owners of these *latifundia*, but brought into being a large section of small squires ready to serve the magnates and helping them to destroy the old institutions based on equality. The old proverb that 'the gentleman on his plot of land is the equal of a lord lieutenant' was out of date when some families possessed standing armies and carried on hereditary feuds.

(iv) that the Legislature was entirely a monopoly of the *szlachta*, as were the law courts and all higher offices in the church. Ministerial posts were nearly all held by members of this class and the king was subject to the advisory authority of the Senate, and his other activities could be nullified by the opposition of the House of Deputies.

(v) that all members of the class were equal before the law and in public life. In Poland there had never been a peerage, and there were no Polish titles. It is true a number of titles were used. A small number of Poles and Lithuanians were descended from the first ruler of Russia, Rurik, the ancestor of all Russian princes, or from Gedymin, the founder of Lithuanian greatness. They were accustomed to use the title of prince. Other titles had been conferred by the Empire and the Papacy, and a few families preserved the tradition that in ancient chronicles they were styled *comites* or *barones* at a time when such titles were fluid. Of all such honorary titles, though used in Polish public life and abroad, Polish law took no cognizance. The title of *szlachcic* or 'gentleman' was to a Pole the highest distinction attainable, and a family's dignity could be enhanced by the number of ancestors who had been senators. This absence of a peerage, together with the number of the class, make it appropriate to translate the word *szlachta* into 'gentry' rather than 'nobility', which for non-Polish readers has the implication of a small peerage or an oligarchy grouped round a strong monarchy.

It is clear that in the early part of the century political power was entirely in the hands of the *szlachta*, but in practice it was held by members of the great families, from which came several good and enlightened statesmen as well as many corrupt and self-seeking officials. The latter were the more formidable in that they could attract the conservative and ignorant members of the lesser gentry to help them in their private feuds and political activities, in the desire to maintain the 'gentleman's paradise' in which they lived. An example of the first type were the members of the Czartoryski family, who as descendants of Gedymin styled themselves princes. An obscure prince of this family had married the daughter of a famous man of letters who was treasurer of Poland. They had two sons, one of whom served under Prince Eugene and married the richest heiress in Poland, the other became Chancellor and the chief statesman of Poland, and a daughter who became the mother of the last king of Poland. The policy of Prince Michael Czartoryski and his brother was one of gradual reform of the constitution and of collaboration with Russia in view of the growing danger from Prussian aggression. He partially succeeded in his efforts to reform the abuses of the constitution, particularly of the *liberum veto*. The main difficulty was that the deputies in the Polish House of Deputies were not free agents but were bound by the mandate of their local assemblies. The *liberum veto* gave a member the right to stop

all public business, not as an individual, but as the representative
of a whole province. This old principle of unanimity (which
survived in the old Russian village communities and in the
English jury system) worked quite well when it was exercised
with judgement and wisdom by educated legislators. In the
seventeenth century, for the first time the *sejm* had been dissolved by this act, and by the eighteenth century political
activity had been reduced to a farce. An enemy or rival of the
ministers, such as a Potocki or a Radziwill, could, by bribery,
induce a humble deputy to put an end to all public business,
with deplorable results to the state. To escape the results of this
weapon Polish ingenuity had evolved another institution: the
Confederation, a body which could be summoned to support
or oppose the ministers and in which the rights of a majority
prevailed. Even a *sejm* could be temporarily converted into a
Confederate *sejm*, in which the *liberum veto* was inoperative.

The reform of the Constitution would not alone have
sufficed to stem the tide of decline. The monopoly of power by
the *szlachta* in the Legislature had prevented the development
of an effective executive body, which, together with the king,
could rule the country and enforce the law. Executive offices
were mainly held by members of the *szlachta*, who had neither
the character nor the knowledge to make them effective
ministers. Sobieski was the last king who had attempted to
rule, and failed completely to master his recalcitrant Legisla-
tures. The king still had considerable powers, but the Saxon
rulers (1697-1763) were quite indifferent to Polish interests
and preferred favourites, who were often of self-seeking and
even despicable character, to the advice of the Czartoryskis.
Such favourites were even prepared to help in the task of
carrying out the Partitions. Poland had no educated body of
diplomats, no legal and financial experts, no civil service, not
even trained soldiers to defend her frontiers. From the time of
the Northern War the Polish country house, whose masters
in the previous century had expelled the Swedes, Russians,
Cossacks and Tartars in desperate fighting, had become re-

signed to the presence of Swedish and Russian armies looting and camping in their territories unchecked.

Finally, the danger of the elective monarchy was becoming greater through the opportunities for interference it gave to aggressive neighbours. The First Partition was made possible by the election as king of a weak member of the *szlachta* by the votes of ignorant deputies instructed by the Russian ambassador at the behest of the Empress, whose lover he had been, with Russian troops in the background. To compensate for this heedlessness of the *szlachta* there was no strong middle-class, and all the peasants were illiterate and mostly serfs. The great bulk of the *szlachta* scarcely realized what was happening and were unable to take any action, owing to the breakdown of the machinery through which alone they could act. Unwittingly they failed to listen to the voices of their wiser leaders and clung to their 'golden freedom', a policy in which they were stoutly supported by Frederick and Catherine.

In this social and political situation change came gradually in the first half of the century. As early as the 'thirties an ex-king, Stanislaw Leszczyński, had written a pamphlet condemning the Polish social and political order. But it was a Piarist Father, Stanislaw Konarski (1700-73), whose practical work in creating a model secondary school in Warsaw, including in its curriculum science and modern languages and inculcating ideals of citizenship, began a process of educational reform, which received an enormous impetus from the acquisition by the state of the large Jesuit estates in the 'seventies. An Educational Commission was established, said to have been the first ministry of the kind in Europe, which set up High Schools, which displaced the old Jesuit establishments. Scholars were found to teach and to supply text-books. Younger members of the *szlachta* joined the commission, like Hugo Kollontaj, who carried out a complete reform of the ancient university of Cracow, of which he became rector. A learned bishop, J. Zaluski, founded a great library; and when a new king, Stanislaw August, succeeded the futile August III, he established a great cultural centre at the court, being himself a former member of Madame Geoffrin's circle and a votary of French enlightenment. Timid as a statesman, he did as much as anyone of his subjects for the cultural revival in Poland, especially in the field of art, poetry, the stage, history and building. Many members of the *szlachta* formed similar cultural centres. A Radziwill princess wrote plays, which were acted in the great palace of Nieświeź. If it was a member of the small middle-class, Staszic, who wrote the greatest works on political and social reform, it was his association with a magnate, the Chancellor Andrew Zamoyski, which enabled him to do so. The spirit in which the re-education of the *szlachta* took place was inspired by two great shocks: the election of a king in 1764 by Russian intrigue, involving the deportation of a number of eminent Poles, including bishops, to Russia, followed by Russian control of the Polish government. The Confederation of Bar, beginning as a movement in defence of the Catholic religion in 1768, became a great national revolt against foreign occupation, in which the *szlachta*, for the first time in the century, displayed as a whole a genuine national sentiment. The second shock was the tragedy of the First Partition, not only showing the truculent and unscrupulous character of the Great Powers, but the complete inability of a once hard-fighting people to make the slightest resistance, not only against the foreigner, but against their own king and a number of corrupt traitors. Deputies in the *sejm* who resisted had to flee for their lives.

Politically helpless, the *szlachta*, shaken out of their complacency and rural seclusion, turned to new leaders, educated in the new schools, who were advocating drastic economic, social and political changes which revolutionized the outlook of the Poles between the First and Second Partitions. The establishment of industries by enterprising landowners was not always successful, but they showed a great advance on the stagnation of the last century and gave a great impetus to the development of a middle-class. Warsaw, a decayed town of

30,000, grew rapidly to be a prosperous city of over 100,000 inhabitants, who began to play some part in the affairs of the country. Many of the landowners began to make improvements in their agricultural methods and to consider the position of their serfs and, in some cases, to give them their freedom. Such a change was made on the estates of Prince Adam Czartoryski, nephew of the former Chancellor. His palace at Pulawy became a great centre of the new ideas and he transmitted to his son, Prince Adam, the education which fitted him to plan with the Emperor Alexander I a new Russia and a revived Polish State, and subsequently keep alive the Polish cause in the darkest years of the nineteenth century.

Ever since the failure of the Czartoryskis to reform the constitution, political questions had been coming more and more to the front in the minds of the country squires, now well educated in the new schools and stirred by the works of Staszic, describing the glories of their past history and emphasizing the need for great reforms to ensure the survival of the Commonwealth. The king, though forced to work in touch with the Russian ambassador, was himself a leader in political discussions. Even the Potockis, the opponents of the Czartoryski family group, represented by the brothers Ignacy and Stanislaw, participated in the planning of a new constitution; and when the great *sejm* of 1788 broached the matter of reform they took the lead in advocating the radical changes, which were suggested by Kollontaj outside the *sejm*. The constitution associated with Russian influence was first overthrown, and an alliance concluded with Prussia. In the great reform concluded in 1791 the progressive party, co-operating with the king and his advisers, carried through the document known as the Constitution of May 3rd, in which the *szlachta* surrendered many of their privileges, and brought forward a new Constitution in which a strong Executive with an hereditary monarchy was associated with a reformed legislature. The middle-class was enfranchised and the serfs taken under the protection of the law. A modern army was created and competent leaders were found including Kościuszko, a young engineer, whose fortification of Saratoga had been one of the decisive events in the victory of the American colonies. The new constitution was regarded as the most liberal of the day and was highly regarded by the Emperor Leopold II and our own Burke. Russia, terrified at the new Polish revival, withdrew her army from Turkey. Prussia betrayed her new ally and the two Powers, assisted by the Polish opponents of the reforms, proceeded to the Second Partition. The Polish liberals set up a Polish government at Cracow under Kościuszko, which recovered much of Poland but was ultimately defeated after a heroic struggle. Poland disappeared as an independent state for 123 years, but the Polish *szlachta* at the end of the century had been transformed into a body of well-educated and patriotic citizens with restored prestige as soldiers, men of learning and strong in every department of administrative, social and political life, destined to play a great part in the events of the next century.

The violent changes that took place in the public life of Poland ending in the partition of the last remnants of the Commonwealth brought about a radical change in the outlook of the *szlachta*. But these changes took place mainly in the towns and in particular in Warsaw. The *szlachta* lived in the wide spaces of the country. Their visits to the city for political purposes were rare and regarded rather as an exciting holiday than as the real business of life. Throughout the century the life of this huge class, possibly numbering 725,000 individuals, changed less than might be expected. They were scattered over the vast territories of the Commonwealth (282,000 square miles before the Partitions), stretching from the Oder nearly to Smolensk and Kiev in the east, from Dantzig and the Baltic seaboard to the Tartar steppe near the Black Sea. An essential element in their lives was their remoteness from the cities and from each other. Foreign travellers are struck by the intolerable roads and lack of accommodation in these lonely areas. Soldiers came for billets and for loot and took little interest in the inhabitants. The historian takes little notice of their life, as all great events happened in the towns, where in Poland decay and disorder were to be seen, but comments on the scandalous life of the demoralized fashionable world, aping the worst side of foreign culture. Even the Polish historian, who was once almost persuaded by members of the Partitioning Powers that his history was a series of blunders, is still apt to expose the treacheries and fantasies of individuals rather than to pay attention to the modest virtues that survived in these remote houses. In the contemporary Polish chronicles, even where great events or the need for reforms are being discussed, we get glimpses of jolly, vigorous, normal activities going on in the background; work on the land, sport in the forests and happy neighbourly meetings varied by occasional feuds. We can find another source to enlighten us on this country life, the epic of the poet Adam Mickiewicz, describing just this society from the outlook of a slightly later generation, but critically, with insight and with great feeling. It is not easy to-day for men accustomed to see civilized life spreading from towns and foreign countries, through the agency of a large and well-trained middle-class, to decayed villages to picture this rural life. The Polish reformers, who had to face the problems of their un-happy state, knew that they must treat them by importing foreign ideas and techniques. This could be done by imitating French civilization – the highest of the time. The king had been in France, dressed like a Frenchman, and strove to impose French manners and literary ideals on his people. By such innovators were the great changes in Poland accomplished. But to most of the country gentry such a man was a figure of fun. Such a man is satirized by Mickiewicz in the Frenchman who terrified his hosts by saying that he means 'to democratize and constitutionalize' them and addresses a beautiful maiden in the kitchen garden in the courtly language of the period, to which she answers in the simple language of a goose girl, which indeed she was. The countryside was in fact divided into two schools of thought about Polish life. The reformers and their followers in such places as Pulawy, the Polish 'Holland House', in their French costumes and manners were stoutly opposed by the conservative masses, who revived the old Polish costumes of the preceding century, with their heads shaved, save for a tuft and long moustaches, and a mode of life which was called 'Sarmatian', a word corresponding to our 'good old Anglo-Saxons'. They were derided by foreigners for carrying a sword, which to them symbolized the traditions of their forefathers, who conquered and converted the pagans of the Baltic coastland, saved Europe from the Tartars and Turks, and even in the last century had driven from their land the invading Swedes, Brandenburgers, Muscovites, Cossacks and Tartars. Though conscious of their glorious military past, they believed that the days of peace had come, and were too remote from realities to realize the need to relearn the art of war. They had a fatal belief in the goodwill of the Great Powers, though they also believed that their system of government was superior to the autocratic and materialistic ideals of their neighbours. This age of pathetic pacifism did not last, not so long as the peaceful time of Victoria between Waterloo and the World Wars. Some of the *szlachta*, especially of the wealthy families. became notorious for their eccentricities. Prince Karol Radziwill (nicknamed 'My dear sir' from his genial manner) was a great figure in the social world of his day, but, like most of his class, his visits to Warsaw, 350 kilometres away, were not frequent. He was Lord-Lieutenant of the great province of Wilno, but most of his life was spent in his great palace at Nieśwież, from which he would travel to the provincial capital Nowogródek for the Sessions or the meeting of the *sejmik*, accompanied by thirty wagons carrying food and other supplies. The Radziwill estates were as large as half of Ireland and their 'court' was far more brilliant than that of the king in Warsaw. He had a large private army and large numbers of small squires who were proud to serve him as servitors in his magnificent palace or managers of his far-flung estates. A stout man of gigantic stature, Prince Karol wore his own fantastic version of the Polish costume and loved fine colours and display. Spoilt as a boy, he grew up to be an impulsive, almost illiterate and capricious character. A great horseman, strong and hardy, he hunted the wild animals of the great forests in all weathers. Once when invited by the king to foxhunting and coursing in Poland he replied: 'Why should I hunt rats and mice in Poland when I can always find boars in Lithuania?' Alert and witty, he was a good master to his dependants and popular on his estates. He ate and drank on a gargantuan scale, was scrupulous in his observance of religious festivals, thoughtful of his gentlemen servitors and devoted to his family. This conduct was sometimes varied by violence where some feud was revived or by fantastic and irresponsible acts for which he was notorious. His attitude to the royal court was one of condescension and his pride in his ancestors tremendous. A less likeable magnate was Felix Potocki, who owned estates of three million acres in the Ukraine. A dour, obstinate and selfish man, whose cruelty contrasted with the joviality of Prince Radziwill, he was disliked and feared by his dependants and continually quarrelling with his equals. His family was traditionally hostile to the Czartoryskis and its members were the chief upholders of 'golden freedom', and were prepared to resort to any methods to preserve it. This led him to collaborate with the Russians in 1792 and leave a name as the greatest traitor in Polish history. From the same family of magnates came two of the great reformers. The eastern provinces, where the peasants were chiefly Lithuanians and Russians in speech, were in the hands of these magnates and the equally great families of Sapieha, Pac, Ogiński, Sanguszko and several others, whose wealth and influence brought them the title of 'little kings', whose feuds disturbed the peace of the countryside, and who had a vested interest in the maintenance of the institutions, which were contributing to the ruin of the Commonwealth. Nevertheless, it was these provinces that produced the great Polish soldier and patriot Kościuszko and the poet Mickiewicz and held the university of Wilno, the rival to the ancient university of Cracow. It is Lithuania which is the scene of the greatest Polish epic.

Although Lithuania was the home of the great eastern magnates, Little Poland, the classic country of the mediaeval magnates, protected by the only Polish mountain range and linked in history with its Hungarian neighbours, still had its great families like those of Tarnowski and Zamoyski. Great Poland, and still more Mazovia, were lands of middle and small estates, and their inhabitants showed less of the oriental glamour of the Ukraine and more of the restrained virtues and moderation of older and more highly developed lands. Here dwelt the typical Polish *szlachcic*, who in the Middle Ages used his christian name and the title of his coat of arms, and later adopted the name of some village or estate with the termination -ski, e.g. Jan of Tarnów became Jan Tarnowski; Henryk of Dombrowa became Henryk Dombrowski. Other families, particularly in the east, took the name of their father with the termination -wicz meaning 'son of', e.g. Mickiewicz means Matthewson.

The mansion of a typical family was built mainly of wood. In a great plain, exposed to foreign attack, men did not build for eternity and the supply of timber was inexhaustible, and, as space cost nothing, the buildings expanded extensively by the addition of new wings and had no upper storey or stairs. Stone and brick came in gradually. The house was usually surrounded by a few trees, generally limes or poplars, which stood up visible over the plain at a great distance. Since the country was flat and monotonous, variety was given to the scene by forests, which also gave the *szlachta* the hunting which was their chief pastime. Life was a mixture of simplicity and display. Hospitality was generously given, visitors bringing their own supplies and often sleeping in mattresses on the floor. On the slightest pretext – a birthday, a festival or a visit – eating and drinking on a large scale took place, followed by dancing, with a complete contempt of time. An old custom was for all the members of a mansion to dress up in fancy costumes and drive in carriages or sledges and visit their friends, who in turn joined them and formed a procession which only ended when all the houses of the locality had been visited. Eating and drinking were taken seriously where supplies of meat, cereals, farmyard products and mead, together with Tokay wine from Hungary, were ample. Such a festival showed a queer mixture of ceremony and easy-going simplicity. In the eastern provinces Cossack, Hussar or Wallach costumes were the fashion for servants, the supply of whom was unlimited. Ceremonial courtesy and dignity were enforced by a strong *patria potestas*. The old gentleman and lady were regarded with awe and affection and the children were brought up with a discipline as severe as that of the servants and serfs. Marriages were generally arranged. The century saw a gradual transition from the 'Sarmatian' fashions to French costumes, but in the background the scene was brightened by the gala costumes of the peasants. On some of the estates the ordinary routine relations of squire and peasant-serf were giving place to more modern ideas of social service. The Czartoryski family led the way in establishing elementary schools, hospitals and model cottages in the villages, but generally the standard of life among the peasants was very low. Wraxall, an English traveller, who never visited a country house, remarks that the peasants often had considerable plots of land and were not as poor as was generally supposed. The relations between squires and serfs varied, but on the whole a patriarchal system worked well unless the squire was a bad master. The more enlightened landowners, towards the end of the century, were preoccupied with the position of the serfs, and some of them converted their status from serfdom to tenancy. The new laws of 1791 improved their position and Kościuszko declared them free, though the Partitioning Powers drove them back into serfdom. The Polish *szlachta* loved their countryside and knew instinctively every aspect of the great plain (*pole*) from which their country took its name. No one has ever expressed the sense of natural beauty more exquisitely than the Polish romantic poets. If a book about eighteenth-century Poland must deal chiefly with great political and national scenes, of great failures and great successes, it should end with some scene like that in which, after a hunt in the forests, the huntsmen gather round the old Tribune who is famous for his horn playing. 'The horn, as a blast of wind, bore the music into the depths of the forest and the echoes repeated the sound. The huntsmen were dumb and the coursers stood still, astounded by the power, the purity, the harmony of the strains. The old man unfolded to the hunters' ears all the art for which he was once famed in the forest. Here he ceased but he held the horn. It seemed to all that the Tribune was playing still, but it was the echo that played.'

10

RUSSIA

Max Beloff

'The appellation of nobility is the result of the qualities and virtues of men who having been foremost in the past, distinguished themselves by their services and turning their very services into merit, acquired for their descendants the distinction of noble birth; are treated as noble all those who either descend from noble ancestors or have received the title from the Monarch in recognition of their deserts.'

Code of Laws of the Russian Empire. Vol. IX. Part I. Par. 15.

THE definition of nobility in Russia which was written into the legal code by the Charter of the Nobility granted by Catherine II in 1785 provides as useful a starting-point as any for an investigation of the status of that class in Russian society in the eighteenth century. For it serves as a reminder of how different was the position enjoyed by the Russian nobility from that which characterized the aristocracies of other European countries with their emphasis on blood and landed-property rather than on service to the state.

The Russian nobility on the eve of the accession of Peter the Great was an amalgam of elements of differing provenance. There were the descendants of the House of Rurik whose principalities had been mediatized with the rise of Moscow and its rulers. There were also the descendants of non-Russian princely families, such as the Jagellons of Lithuania, and descendants of Tartar princes, whose lands had been absorbed with the expansion of the Russian Empire from the fifteenth century onwards. In the eighteenth century there were to be further additions from this source. But also there were the descendants of those families which had made up the court

following of the mediaeval princes in whose highest rank stood
the Boyars – although the personal title of boyar is not strictly
speaking one of nobility.

Although such families possessed hereditary estates, their
chances of forming an aristocratic caste which might have
challenged the authority of the ruler were weakened by a
number of things particular to Russia, not least the absence of
any system of primogeniture. The inescapable tendency of
estates towards subdivision, while titles of nobility were transmitted to an ever-increasing number of a noble's descendants,
forced them into a dependence upon the Tsar for further grants
of lands and of serfs. Such lands, whether granted to existing
noble families or to new men who had earned them through
service to the Tsar, were not allodial like the earlier estates but
granted as a direct return for such services. Ivan IV not only
built up a rival class of service nobility but completed the
humiliation of the mediatized princes by forcing them to
exchange their hereditary allodial possessions for more distant
estates held on service tenure. In this way, from the earliest
period of the modern Russian Empire, the noble class was
distinguished from the aristocracy of other countries by the
enforcement upon it of obligations to the State, especially in
the military sphere that had long been obsolete in the West, and
also by the lack of any specific connection between particular
families and particular estates. The land and those who tilled
it, who were increasingly assimilated in the seventeenth and
early eighteenth centuries into a single class of serfs, were
thought of merely as producing revenue, not as a source of
social prestige or political influence. The castles of mediaeval
feudatories and the great country houses that succeeded them in
the West were absent from the Russian scene, where the lack of
natural stone was an obstacle to their construction in any case;
and territorial titles were also lacking.

The nobility failed to take advantage of the 'time of troubles'
at the beginning of the seventeenth century following upon
the extinction of the old ruling house. Michael Romanov was

indeed eventually chosen as the new Tsar because a member of some more eminent family might have been too powerful; and he was for a time compelled to work in concert with the Boyars. But the internecine rivalries of the different princely houses prevented any advance of the nobility as a class and the autocracy was firmly re-established. These conflicts which so weakened the nobility revolved round the principle which can only be represented by the untranslatable Russian word 'myestnichestvo'. This was the practice of ranking families in a strict order of precedence according to the precedence held by their ancestors on recorded occasions. No Russian noble would serve under the command of another if the latter's ancestor had at some time served under his. This rule was so little conducive to military efficiency that in 1682 it was formally abolished by the Tsar Theodore, who for better security consigned to the flames the books in which the order of precedence was recorded. Henceforward all nobles were to be formally equal and the heraldic chamber of the senate was appointed to revise the 'velvet book' or register of the nobility which it was intended should now be closed against new additions.

In the history of the nobility, as in so much else in Russia, the reign of Peter the Great is of crucial importance. But the process which he carried forward had begun earlier. The two existing forms of landed property, the allodial and the feudal (if the terms are permissible), were assimilated to each other. There were some difficulties involved in making the service-lands hereditary, since the sons of a landowner of this class might not have completed their stint of service before his death; but a decree of 1684, passed, that is to say, during Peter's minority, provided that in such cases direct heirs at least might inherit. By Peter's time there was virtually only one class of landed property: all lands were hereditary and all carried the burden of service. The real distinction was not between the old and the new nobility, but between the nobility of the capital and that of the provinces, the former paying by more arduous service and the dangers of proximity to court for its greater share of political influence. But Peter's purpose of modernizing Russia, at least in its military and administrative aspects, meant further changes. The old obligation upon nobles to appear in arms when called for, with an appropriate number of followers, had to give way to a system of direct conscription under which the obligation of the noble was to serve as an officer. For those unsuitable for, or past the age of, military service and for other qualified persons outside the ranks of the existing nobility there was service of a civilian kind to be performed.

To perform all these functions it was Peter's intention to create a single class partaking both of the character of a bureaucracy and of an aristocracy, since it could only be maintained by the possession of lands and serfs, and would be marked out from the rest of the population by its exemption from the poll-tax and from the normal machinery of recruitment. To this class the Polish-derived name of 'schliachetstvo' was rather incongruously given. Since it exercised important functions of justice and police and was responsible for the peasants' taxes, the nobility was directly interested in the final hardening of the bonds of serfdom, and the final interposition of itself between the serfs in private hands – something over half the population of Russia by the middle of the eighteenth century – and the state. But its burdens were heavy.

Under Peter, service began at fifteen and was for life. Since there was a preference for civil as against military service, it was provided that not more than one-third of a family could serve in a civil capacity. By the decree of 1714 which finally wiped out even the formal differentiation between allodial and feudal holdings, Peter introduced the practice of entailing estates upon a single heir, though the right was given of choosing which son was to benefit by this, and primogeniture was not insisted upon. By this means it seemed as though nobles who had been able to avoid service by retreating to their share of the patrimonial estates would no longer be able to do so, and this helps to explain the unpopularity of the decree with the nobility which from the beginning did its best to evade it.

The system of service was given form by the famous edict of 1722 by which all the servants of the crown were divided into fourteen orders or 'tchin' rising in two parallel ladders, civil and military, from the registry clerk and ensign at the bottom to the chancellor and field-marshal at the top. The various ranks on the civil side denoted status, not function, and their designations borrowed from the German were quite meaningless. The eight top ranks carried with them hereditary nobility, and the last six personal non-hereditary noble rank.

This arrangement led during the eighteenth century to a steady inflation in the numbers of nobles, who were reckoned by the British Ambassador Lord Macartney, in the 1760's, to number with their families half a million persons out of a total population of twenty-eight million. The same figure of half a million was arrived at by another foreigner, the soldier of fortune Baron von Manstein, for a period about two decades earlier, when he gave a much lower estimate for the total population. Peter further added to the numbers of the nobility by being the first Russian sovereign to create titles. His favourite Menshikov was the first Russian, other than the descendants of the appanage princes of the house of Rurik to acquire the title of prince. And he also introduced into Russia, the previously unknown titles of count and baron. A precedent was created also for the ennoblement of those distinguished by their economic services with the admission to personal rank as a noble of the great ironmaster of the Urals, Nikita Demidov, in 1720. His family became hereditary nobles in 1725.

Some Russian historians have taken the view that before the time of Peter the country had no official class or aristocracy with a sentiment of separation from the mass of the people. However that may be, the Russian nobility of the eighteenth century were separated not only in law but in outlook, habits, dress and even language from the remainder of the people. Speaking German or French – the latter dominant at court from the middle of the century – they participated in the luxury of a court so reckless that it astounded even those acquainted with the ostentation of the French. 'It would be difficult', wrote a foreign visitor to Russia in the reign of the Empress Anne, 'to determine whether this ostentation is the effect of the government of women who are naturally fond of show and dress, rather than the consequence of the administration of foreigners, who by this means impoverish the natives of the country.' The fact that it continued even after Anne's German favourites gave way to the more national Russian atmosphere of Elizabeth's court is an argument against the latter suggestion. But this very luxury was found in juxtaposition with barbaric filth. The enforced residence of the great nobles at Peter's new capital on the Neva ran them into huge expense for palaces that were with difficulty maintained against the rigours of the climate and the unsuitability of the site. To quote Count Algarotti again: 'Their walls are all cracked quite out of perpendicular, and ready to fall. It has been wittily enough said that ruins make themselves in other places, but that they were built at Petersburg.'

It would be too much to suggest that the Petrine social structure proved as fragile as the palaces of his nobles, but it is clear that the succeeding generations saw a strong and partially successful reaction against the burden which he had placed upon the shoulders of the nobility. Their duties to serve the state and to educate themselves – and in many respects service was the only real form of education available – were not denied in principle: but the elements of compulsion and permanence were resented and combated. In this sphere notable successes were achieved: on the other hand, attempts at turning the nobility into a closed caste and at capturing for it a defined share of political power were fruitless. The Russian State remained an autocracy, and the successful interventions of the nobles were confined to the use of the Guards regiments to depose an unpopular autocrat, or to influence the order of succession.

Once again, as in the seventeenth century, it was the divisions among the nobles that proved their undoing. But these divisions no longer took the form of rivalries between particular individuals or families in the first instance, but rather of a clash of interests between particular groups within the increasingly broad framework of the nobility at large. The nature of these divisions does not always appear with great clarity. Earlier historians have made much of the division between the old families of the pre-Petrine nobility and those who had worked their way up through the 'tchin'. More recent historians have divided them according to economic criteria, declaring that there was a great and growing difference between the greater nobles, the aristocracy proper, many of whom, particularly after the middle of the century, were directly interested in the new industrial and commercial currents of the age, and the lesser nobles maintained wholly by the revenues of their traditionally-managed small estates. This distinction would seem to have replaced that between the nobles of the capital and those of the provinces, seeing that Peter's reforms had drawn all except perhaps the most impoverished into a single system of service and rewards. It is probable that these differing interests all played their parts in the several critical junctures of the remainder of the eighteenth century.

The main apparent opportunity for an assertion of political claims by the nobility arose on the death of Peter II in 1730 when the Supreme Privy Council set up in 1726 decided upon Anne, the niece of Peter I, as the new sovereign. The dominant figure at the time was Dmitri Mikhailovich Golitsyn, a member of one of the leading families among the old nobility. He proposed that the new Empress should be obliged on her accession to agree to a series of consitutional 'Articles' based upon those forced upon the Swedish monarchy in 1720.

The 'Articles' stipulated that Anne (the widow of the Duke of Courland) should not remarry nor name her successor: in other words, the Russian monarchy was to become elective like that of Poland. A Supreme Council of eight dignitaries was to be permanently attached to the sovereign, and without its consent the Empress was neither to declare war, make peace nor levy new taxes. Its consent was to be requisite for the conferment of any high military rank, for the disposal of crown lands and the spending of public funds. It was to control the armed forces, and without its consent no noble was in future to be deprived of life, property or honours without trial. Algarotti's comment that in the midst of so many troops (to whom indeed Anne owed her crown) the Russian people had been seized with 'a fit of liberty' might hardly seem too strong.

In fact, however, the 'Articles' are of interest only as showing the kind of thing which one section of the nobility had in mind. Among the lesser nobility some wanted more far-reaching constitutional innovations which would have given them a defined rôle alongside their superiors: others simply preferred the traditional autocracy. Their views could not be ignored, particularly since Moscow was full of nobles who had come there for the funeral of Peter II. But Golitsyn would not go far enough to meet those who wanted some share in political control to win much support.

When Anne arrived in Moscow from her home at Mitau on the Baltic, the partisans of absolutism found it easy to exploit the differences among the nobles. It was clear that what most of them were concerned for was not political power but a return to the more favourable personal position which they and their families had enjoyed before the reforms of Peter the Great. This meant limiting the duration of service, abolishing the decree of Peter which prevented them parcelling out their estates among their heirs, and the granting of the right for nobles to enter the army directly as officers without passing through the ranks. It was only necessary to suggest that the new Empress would be prepared to grant these wishes of her own free will once she was given the rights of her predecessors for the constitutionalists to lose most of their support. Anne publicly denounced the 'Articles' and was acclaimed as absolute sovereign. Manstein's verdict on these events is not surprising: 'I much doubt', he wrote, 'whether this empire, or rather the higher nobility, will ever achieve their liberty. The lesser nobility, who are extremely numerous in Russia, will constantly oppose great obstacles to it, being more afraid of the tyranny of a number of the great than of the power of a single sovereign.'

The hopes placed in Anne by the nobles were not disappointed. In 1731, the effort to enforce entails was abolished, and apart from a few families who had private settlements of their own, the Russian nobility returned to its former practice of dividing up estates equally among the heirs. In the same year a corps of cadets was established to enable noblemen's sons to enter the Guards regiments as fully-fledged officers. This went some way towards satisfying the demands of the nobles that if they were obliged to undergo education, it should not be in company with commoners. In the same spirit, in 1755, a separate *gymnasium* was set up for the sons of nobles in Moscow. And in the same year the nobles objected to the establishment of a university at Moscow, on the ground that the sons of nobles might be forced to attend the same classes as the sons of bourgeois.

More important was the abolition in 1736 of universal and permanent state service. Henceforth the period of service was limited to twenty-five years beginning at the age of twenty, and if a father had more than one son, one could be freed of his obligations so as to look after the family's estate. Even so, the unpopularity of service did not diminish. When peace was made with the Turks in 1739 an attempt was made to reduce the number of generals in the army by permitting the retirement of all officers with above twenty years' service. But so many officers tried to take advantage of this order, so Manstein tells us, that the edict was rescinded.

It must not be thought that Anne's legislation meant that she accepted in full the pretensions of the nobility. Her own rule was carried on largely through her German favourites, and she showed notorious contempt for the Russian aristocracy, choosing scions of three famous and ancient houses as her court fools. Nor in that barbaric court was the office of fool a sinecure.

Indeed throughout the changes which took place during the century, one thing remained constant: the lack of respect paid in Russia to noble birth as such. To western observers this was a permanent source of wonder. Lord Macartney wrote: 'All nobles are equal and have precedence only according to the rank of their employment in the state: thus a common writer or common soldier, though of the best extraction, if he rises either in the civil or military, takes the place of every person whatsoever of an inferior character, though sprung from the first families of the empire.'

By the time that Macartney wrote, however, the greatest change of all had taken place: the abolition of compulsory service altogether. Under Elizabeth the economic privileges of the nobility had grown, and the Senate, a channel for the political influence of the great nobles, had acquired new powers. But possibly the most important aspect of her reign, even from the point of view of the country's interior development, was Russia's participation in the Seven Years War. Not for the last time in Russian history, the officers of her victorious armies returned to Russia after experiencing at first hand the attractions of countries on a much higher material and cultural level. Since these officers were nobles, this episode meant in fact the introduction into the only educated class in Russian society of new, not to say revolutionary, ideas. From this date there begins, one might argue, the history of the Russian *intelligentsia* which in its origins was necessarily mainly an offshoot of the nobility.

The legislation which marked the ill-starred reign of Elizabeth's successor, Peter III, in 1762, added to the effect of the war by permitting Russians freely to travel abroad. But this was overshadowed at the time by the fact that Peter, in order to win political support, also abolished all compulsory service for the nobility except in times of grave national danger. It is true that the effect of this must not be over-estimated. Service to the

State in some form continued to be the normal practice among Russian noblemen. It was encouraged by the State, for instance by sumptuary laws which discriminated in favour of nobles who had done their stint. Nobles who had not served were not received at court. And the idea that compulsory service could be reimposed seems to have lingered on. At least we learn from the charming childhood memoirs of Serge Aksakov that in the very last decade of the century it was still possible to tease the small son of a Russian noble by telling him that compulsory service had been reimposed, and that he would have to leave his family and go off to serve the Tsar. On the other hand, we learn from contemporaries that there was at once in 1762 a great exodus from the capital of nobles going off to look after their own estates. And from this time onwards, there is clearly a provincial society in Russia, whereas before such society had been confined to women, children, old men and the poorest and most ignorant of the noble class. There were still Russian nobles at this time who were illiterate. By 1773, Catherine II noted that most Russian nobles lived in the country. Although the Russian nobility never became a rural aristocracy, they did develop local interests and a corporate feeling which had a profound effect on the later developments of Catherine's reign. Provincial town life which had been largely limited to the activities of Russia's backward merchant class could now move forward. We may perhaps think of it reproducing on a minor scale what a German observer noted of Moscow at the end of the century. He found there that its population varied tremendously between summer and winter, since of some 6360 noble families with houses in Moscow, 5000 left it in the summer months for their country estates. With their dependants and servants this meant an annual exodus of about 120,000 persons from a total population of about 420,000.

The higher aristocracy in Catherine's reign did not take part in this movement towards the provinces. Political intrigue and the glamour of the court held it at the capital. Its sense of class superiority was hardened; and a new emphasis was laid upon the antiquity of its genealogies. It tried to secure educational institutions for itself, just as the nobility as a whole had tried to keep clear in this sphere of all bourgeois contacts. It tried to prevent any further additions to the nobility and put forward the theory that Peter's system of 'tchin' had been intended only as a temporary measure. In Little Russia, the Ukraine, where a new nobility and a new serfdom had grown up after the Russian conquest, its pretensions under Polish influence were even more extreme. But its demand to have a Siberian nobility created was unsuccessful.

The economic foundations of the Russian nobility became more varied also as the century progressed. Despite the essential privilege which they enjoyed of owning land and serfs – a privilege fortified by the legislation of Anne and Elizabeth – and despite the acquisition of other sources of incidental profit such as the monopoly of distilling, which they got under Peter III, the Russian nobles never managed as a whole to develop into an important agency of economic enterprise or to advance. Their wealth when acquired, often through the lavish bounty of their Sovereigns, especially their female Sovereigns, was spent on personal comfort and luxury, and not invested.

Their history shows a remarkable parallelism with that of another ruling agrarian class, the American Southern planter aristocracy of the next century. In both cases the dominant factor in their fortunes was the steady rise in prices resulting from an increased external demand for their produce. In both cases land was relatively plentiful and the rise in prices was mainly reflected in rising labour costs. Just as the price of the 'prime field hand' in the Cotton Kingdom rose with the price of cotton, so the price of the Russian serf rose in the course of the eighteenth century, threefold perhaps by the middle of the century and almost double again by its end. But the rise in prices had not been the doing of the landlord and did not for the most part stimulate him to further efforts. Even if they lived on their estates, the Russian nobles did nothing to emulate the improving landlords of eighteenth-century England. When in the second half of the century mortgage banks were set up for their use, the money raised was again spent on consumption. Where they differed from the Southern planter was in their conviction that the State owed them employment and a living, and in their readiness to accept its dictates.

Under Peter the Great the beginnings of Russian manufacture were partly a matter of state enterprise and partly the result of the activities of merchants or of nobles. The latter benefited from the fact that until the edict of 1721 (which was not apparently used a great deal by the merchants, its intended beneficiaries), they alone could make use of serf labour. And factories were set up on noble estates, either under direct management, or let out to serfs on the payment of rent. Nobles also formed some of the companies which took over from the State certain of the enterprises initiated by Peter. But in this period they were only responsible for a small proportion of the total number of the country's industrial enterprises.

In the latter part of the century, manufactures owned by nobles increased in number. And it must not be overlooked that the nobility absorbed some of the more important non-noble entrepreneurs, such as the metallurgists, the Davidov and Yakovlev families. But in the great iron industry of the Urals the hereditary nobles were slow to take part. It was only in the 'fifties that the great local landowners, the Stroganovs, turned their attention from their old monopoly of salt-mining to metallurgy; at about the same time, the State handed over at low cost through the operation of court influence a number of its own metallurgical enterprises in the area. Later for the same reason it bought some of them back for larger sums. Nobles thus took part in the expansion of the Ural industrial complex southwards, but with little success against the competition of more mobile and enterprising commercial capital. Even the final step on the part of the State, the abandonment in 1782 of its claim to the ownership of all mineral wealth in favour of the proprietors of the soil – a claim maintained since 1719 – did not change the general picture. In the non-metallurgical industries also the merchants got over the handicap, imposed upon them after the legislation of 1746, 1758 and 1762, of not being able to use serf-labour, and continued to be the dominant element. This failure of the nobility to adapt itself to the economic diversification of the country along with its growing differentiation is seen by economic historians as the main cause of the crisis in the nobility's fortunes in the reign of Catherine II.

To some extent the interpretation of the place of the nobility in Catherine II's reign will depend upon one's assessment of the policies of that enigmatic monarch. The traditional view has been that it was a reign in which the nobility reached, with the assent of the Sovereign, the peak of its rise to privilege and influence. More recent inquiries suggest that Catherine's real intention was to free the monarchy from the threat which the nobility seemed to present at the beginning of her reign and to make use, for this purpose, of the growing differentiation already mentioned between different sections of the noble class. This differentiation can most clearly be seen in relation to the number of serfs owned by members of different groups among the nobility. Thanks to the continued subdivision of estates, some, we are told, were left with no serfs and had to work their own fields. Of the rest, it has been estimated that in 1777 32 per cent of the nobles owned less than ten serfs each; 27 per cent owned between ten and twenty; 25 per cent between twenty and one hundred; and 16 per cent over one hundred. The trend seems to have been towards the growth of the very largest estates. These large landowners were interested in their estates from the point of view of selling their produce, while the lesser landowners regarded their lands as the foundation of a subsistence economy furnishing them directly with maintenance.

In Elizabeth's reign there had already been signs that some of the larger landowners understood that they had a certain community interest with the merchant class, who were profiting by the growth of Russia's foreign trade. They may have

helped to secure the régime of internal free trade which came
into effect in Russia in the 1750's, and were prepared to see
merchants allowed to buy land and even, under certain circumstances, to own serfs. Where they themselves were not primarily
interested in the produce of serf labour, they were prepared to
consider limitations on serfdom itself and even to look to its
ultimate abolition. In the sphere of foreign policy the large
landowners and merchants were in favour of expansion to the
Black Sea, which would open up new markets in Southern
Europe and break the traditional hold of foreign merchants on
the commerce of Russia's northern ports. The lesser nobles,
whose estates lay, for the most part, in the north of the country,
found these measures unattractive and provided the real impetus behind the demand for consolidating the privileges of
their order against both merchants and peasants.

Catherine's early years were dominated by her fear for the
security of her throne, which she owed to a conspiracy between
part of the upper aristocracy and the lesser nobles of the Guards
regiments. At the outset of her reign, she rejected, after some
hesitation, the suggestion made by Panin of a permanent
council of nobles as an element in the governmental structure,
since she saw in it a possible check on her own autocracy. In
1763 she began a reduction of the powers of the senate to the
more modest scale of Anne's reign. In the same year a Commission was called together to revise the decree of Peter III
abolishing compulsory service, but although there was no
prospect of its restoration, it was made clear that the intention
was to encourage voluntary service to the crown. At least one
member of the Commission suggested further extensions of
the personal privileges of the nobles as against the crown on
the one hand and the peasantry on the other, and even suggested a corporative organisation for the nobility, thus foreshadowing the charter of 1785; but the nobles clearly did not
contemplate any more than the crown the ending of their
intimate participation in government. The report of the Commission was accepted by Catherine but no laws were promul-

gated at the time. In the next few years a number of decrees did appear assenting to some of the claims made by the nobles as against the peasantry and the merchants.

The argument as to Catherine's policy turns largely on the interpretation given to the Legislative Commission of 1767-8 and to the document presented by Catherine to that body and known as the 'Instruction'. The interpretation of this document as an early essay in liberalism has lately been disputed. And contemporary accounts by foreigners can be quoted for the view that Catherine's main purpose in calling together a representative body was to secure a new fundamental law assuring her own position and that of her son. It has been suggested that the Commission itself, which contained 160 nobles as against as many as 207 representatives of the urban middle-class, took this form because the electoral machinery was designed to prevent the nobles having a majority. It has also been suggested that the Instruction was drawn up without the thought, originally, of any such representative body considering it; and its early drafts can be used to show that Catherine modified the views of her admitted model, Montesquieu, precisely on the point of the position of the nobility. It was the bureaucracy, not the nobility, which was to be the intermediary power between crown and people.

The outlook of the representatives of the nobles in the Commission of 1767 was different from that which they had displayed in 1763. The five years of active provincial life had given them a new corporate sense and the very business of coming together to elect representatives to the Commission gave them the opportunity of common action for the first time. The demands which they brought from their constituencies were various. Some showed a wish to lighten the burdens on the serfs, and only a minority wished to extend the rights of the landlords. They demanded reform of the courts and the election of judges by the nobles, and in some cases the election of administrative officers for the affairs of the nobility. Out of the 158 sets of instructions, twenty-three gave some place to elective organs.

These demands were largely achieved along with other traditional ones in the charter of 1785. By this charter the nobles were assured of freedom from compulsory service, direct taxation, corporal punishment and the billeting upon them of troops; they were now permitted freely to dispose of their lands, of mineral rights and other sources of wealth; they were given the right to establish industrial enterprises on their estates and to trade their products both inside the country and abroad, to hold fairs and markets on their lands and to possess house property in the towns. Nobility was to be hereditary and no noble could be deprived of his rank except by the judgement of the court for some dishonourable crime. In such a court a noble could only be judged by a jury of his peers and a regular trial was necessary before he could be deprived of his life, property or honours.

The same charter set up a corporative organization for the nobility. Each province was to have its own corps of nobles with its constituted officers, and this body would provide the functionaries for local government as well as having the right to petition the Senate and the crown and to perform certain duties in connection with the noble class itself. The nobility, for this purpose, was divided into six classes but each was given the same right of vote. For this reason the upper aristocracy took no part in the provincial affairs and preferred to look after its interests in the capital. For this and other reasons the new organization was more imposing than effective. The functionaries chosen by the nobility were no less subservient to the autocracy than directly nominated officials. Indeed, while some Russian historians have applauded the scheme as giving the nobility a worth-while occupation after their freedom from the obligation to serve, others have treated it simply as a burden imposed upon the nobles by the crown in place of that which had been removed. As regards the personal privileges, the fact that most of them required specific statement at all in the last quarter of the eighteenth century is indicative of the social backwardness of Russia. The nobles of that country seemed in 1785 to want little more than what free men generally possessed in most of the rest of Europe. However one may interpret the policies of Catherine, the nobility, at the end of the eighteenth century, was no less a subservient element in the Russian State than it had been under the masterful Peter one hundred years before.

SELECT BIBLIOGRAPHIES

1. ENGLAND

BECAUSE there is no English 'noblesse', there is no single systematic study of our subject. The most illuminating treatment is in the first chapter of L. B. Namier's *England in the Age of the American Revolution* (1930), and the whole of this work and the same author's *The Structure of Politics at the Accession of George III* (2 vols., 1929) contain indispensable material. A. S. Turberville, *The House of Lords in the XVIIIth Century* (1927), *The House of Lords in the Age of Reform, 1784-1837* (1958), and the same author's article, 'The Younger Pitt and the House of Lords', *History*, vol. XXI (1937), are the main authorities on the peerage. G. E. Mingay, *English Landed Society in the Eighteenth Century* (London, 1963) contains a full treatment of the subject and also has much useful bibliographical information. T. H. Hollingsworth, *The Demography of the British Peerage* (Supplement to *Population Studies*, vol. XVIII, no. 2) includes much new data about the marriages, fertility and mortality of this group.

Among studies of individual families, three are particularly valuable: G. Scott-Thomson, *The Russells in Bloomsbury, 1669-1771* (1940); A. S. Turberville, *A History of Welbeck Abbey and its Owners* (2 vols., 1936); Hon. H. A. Wyndham, *A Family History, 1688-1837: the Wyndhams of Somerset, Sussex, and Wiltshire* (1950). There are a large number of collections of letters which shed light on the social life of the aristocracy and gentry. These are conveniently listed in Section IX of D. J. Medley and S. Pargellis, *Bibliography of British History in the Eighteenth Century*. The most comprehensive is *Horace Walpole's Correspondence*, ed. by W. S. Lewis (16 vols. in progress 1937–). The following are also very informative: *Verney Letters of the Eighteenth Century*, ed. by Margaret Maria, Lady Verney (2 vols., 1930); *Purefoy Letters, 1735-1753*, ed. by G. Eland (2 vols., 1931); *The Pembroke Papers, 1734-1780*, ed. by Lord Herbert (1939); *Lord Hervey and His Friends, 1726-1738*, ed. by the Earl of Ilchester (1950). There is considerable information about the social and economic position of the gentry in a relatively advanced industrial area in

Edward Hughes's *North Country Life in the Eighteenth Century* (1952). See also Edward Hughes, *North Country Life in the Eighteenth Century*, Vol. II. *Cumberland and Westmoreland, 1700–1830* (Oxford, 1965). The best elementary introduction to the strict settlement is Sir Frederick Pollock's *The Land Laws*; see also H. J. Habakkuk, 'Marriage Settlements in the Eighteenth Century', *Trans. Roy. Hist. Soc.*, 4th ser., vol. XXXII (1950). *The Village Labourer*, by J. L. and B. Hammond, is one-sided, but it is still very stimulating in its observations on the landowning class.

An immense amount of raw material is contained in the standard genealogical works. G. E. Cockayne, *The Complete Peerage*, new edn. rev. and much enlarged by the Hon. Vicary Gibbs, H. Arthur Doubleday and others (1910– in progress). This does not include children and collaterals, who are to be found in Arthur Collins, *The Peerage of England* (edn. of 1812 ed. by Sir Egerton Brydges, 9 vols.); G. E. Cockayne, *Complete Baronetage* (1900–6); Burke's *Genealogical and Heraldic History of the Landed Gentry* (15th edn., 1937), ed. by H. Pirie-Gordon.

2. FRANCE

H. Carré, *La Noblesse de France et l'opinion publique au XVIIIᵉ siècle* (1920), deals directly with the subject. There are many histories of French society in the eighteenth century (e.g. by M. Kovalewsky (1909–11), H. Sée (1924, 1946), L. Ducros (E.T. 1926)). The most recent and most useful is P. Sagnac, *La Formation de la société française moderne* (2 vols., 1945–6). M. Marion, *Dictionnaire des institutions de la France au 17ᵉ et 18ᵉ siècles* (1923), gives information on technical points.

Genealogies may be traced in F. A. Aubert de La Chesnaye-Desbois and Badier, *Dictionnaire de la noblesse* (3rd edn., 19 vols., 1863), and in P. L. Laine, *Archives généalogiques et historiques de la noblesse de France* (11 vols., 1841). There are other similar compilations; none are exhaustive, and reference must be made in the cases of some families to works of a local character, e.g. E. de Magny, *Nobliaire de Normandie* (2 vols., 1889). Concerning rank and precedence, see Guyot, *Traité des droits . . . annexes en France à chaque dignité* (4 vols., 1787), and the *Mémoires du Duc de Luynes*, ed. L. Dussieux and E. Soulie (17 vols., 1860). On forged titles of nobility: H. Chobaut, 'Un "Fabricant" de nobles en 1789' (*Annales historiques de la Révolution française*, 1939). For the revival of the nobility of Corsica: A. Chuquet, *La Jeunesse de Napoléon*, vol. 1 (1892). For the *noblesse dorée*: Britsch, *La Jeunesse de Philippe Égalité* (1926); P. Filleul, *Le Duc de Montmorency-Luxembourg* (1939); R. Dauvergne, *Les Résidences du Maréchal de Croy* (1718-84) (1950). The brilliant life of high society is well chronicled in the many works of E. and J. de Goncourt; also by G. Maugras and P. de Nolhac. For the higher clergy: A. Sicard, *L'Ancien Clergé de France. Les Évêques avant la Révolution* (5th edn., 1912). For intendants: F. Dumas, *La Généralité de Tours au XVIIIe siècle. L'Intendant Du Cluzel, 1766-83* (1894); and Ardescheff, *Les Intendants de Province sous Louis XVI* (1909). For magistrates of the Parlement of Paris: E. Dard, *Hérault de Séchelles, 1759-94* (1907); G. Michon, *Essai sur l'histoire du parti feuillant. Adrien Duport* (1924); for those of the provincial parlements: J. Egret, *Le Parlement de Dauphiné et les affaires publiques dans la deuxième moitié du XVIIIe siècle* (2 vols., 1942); A. Colombet, *Les Parlementaires bourguignons à la fin du XVIIIe siècle* (1937); Le Moy, *Le Parlement de Bretagne et le pouvoir royal au XVIIIe siècle* (1909). For the poor nobility: P. de Vaïssière, *Gentilshommes campagnards de l'ancienne France* (1925); Chateaubriand, *Mémoires d'outre-tombe*, ed. Levaillant, vol. 1 (1947). For a family average in fortune, but in no other respect: de Loménie, *Les Mirabeau* (5 vols., 1891).

Concerning nobles in the army, the discussion in the monographs (Mention, Tuetey, Hartmann) is brought to a point in E. G. Léonard, 'La Question sociale dans l'armée française au XVIIIe siècle', *Annales, économies, sociétés, civilisations* (1948), while A. Babeau, *La Vie militaire sous l'ancien régime* (2 vols., 1890), is full of picturesque detail. Questions concerning the economic activities of the nobility are summarized in H. Lévy-Bruhl, 'La Noblesse de France et le commerce à la fin de l'ancien régime', *Revue d'histoire moderne* (1933). On enclosures, see M. Bloch in *Annales, économies, sociétés, civilisations* (1930), and on the forests of Franche-Comté, L. Mazoyer (*ibid.*, 1932).

It is impossible to refer here to the many works on the movement of ideas in the eighteenth century (Mornet, Viatte, etc.). A. Monglond, *Le Préromantisme français* (2 vols., 1930), is particularly suggestive, and G. Bonno, *La Constitution britannique devant l'opinion française de Montesquieu à Bonaparte* (1931), and E. Carcassonne, *Montesquieu et le problème de la constitution française au XVIIIe siècle* (1927), give the development of constitutional ideas. On Vauvenargues see F. Vial (1938). For the effect of the Revolution on the ideas of the nobility see F. Baldensperger, *Le Mouvement des idées dans l'émigration française, 1789-1815* (2 vols., 1924). Since this essay was written the following important volumes have been published: Franklin L. Ford, *Robe and Sword: the Regrouping of the French Aristocracy after Louis XIV* (Harvard, 1952); and Robert Forster, *The Nobility of Toulouse in the Eighteenth Century: a Social and Economic Study* (Johns Hopkins, 1960). See also E. G. Léonard, *L'armée et ses problèmes au XVIIIe siècle* (Paris, 1958); F. Bluche, *Les Magistrats du Parlement de Paris au XVIIIe siècle (1715-1771)* (Paris, 1960) and the following articles—M. Reinhard, 'Elite et Noblesse dans la seconde moitié du XVIIIe siècle', *Revue d'Histoire Moderne et Contemporaine*, iii (1956), 13-19; F. Bluche, 'L'origine sociale du personnel ministériel Français au XVIIIe siècle', *Bulletin de la Société d'Histoire Moderne* (1957), 9-13; R. Forster, 'The Provincial Noble: A Reappraisal', *American Historical Review*, lxviii (1962-3); B. Behrens, 'Privileges and taxes in France at the end of the Ancien Régime', *Economic History Review*, 2nd ser. XV (1963), 451-75, and A. Goodwin, 'The Social Origins and privileged status of the French eighteenth-century nobility', *Bulletin of the John Rylands Library*, Vol. 47 (1965), 382-403.

3. SPAIN

R. Altamira y Crevea, *Historia de España*, vol. IV, 5th edn. (Barcelona, 1935).
A. Benavides, *Órdenes de cabellería* (1864).
Gerald Brenan, *The Spanish Labyrinth: the Social and Political Background of the Civil War*, 2nd edn. (Cambridge, 1950).
Conde de Campomanes, *Memorial ajustado del Expediente Consultivo para una ley agraria* (1784).
Francisco de Cárdenas, *Ensayo sobre la historia de la propriedad territorial en España*, vol. II (Madrid, 1875).
G. Desdevises du Dézert, *L'Espagne de l'ancien régime* (revised in *Revue Hispanique*, 1926, -27, -28).
F. Fernández de Béthencourt, *Historia genealógica* (1897).
G. M. de Jovellanos, *Informe sobre la ley agraria* (1787); *Memorial de 1784* (printed *Boletín Acad. de Hist.*, 1914).
R. Leonhard, *Agrarpolitik und Agrarreform in Spanien unter Karl III* (Munich, 1909).
A. Morel-Fatio, *Études sur l'Espagne*, Deuxième Série (Paris, 1890).
Marqués del Saltillo, *La nobleza en el pasado* (Madrid, 1930).

J. Sarrailh, *La Crise religieuse en Espagne à la fin du XVIIIᵉ siècle* (Oxford, 1951).

J. Sempere y Guarinos, *Historia de los vínculos y mayorazgos* (1805).

Of the many addresses and pamphlets of the Economic Societies the best is *Discurso para la abertura de las Juntas Generales que celebro la Sociedad Basconcada en la Villa de Vergara* (1785).

The best foreign accounts are those of Bourgoing, Clarke, Townshend, Moldenhauer (in *Revue Hispanique*, vol. LXIX), Court life in *The Spanish Journals of Elizabeth Lady Holland*, ed. Ilchester, (London, 1910) and *The Journals and Correspondence of Lord Auckland*, vol. II (London, 1861). Arcos's protest to Philip V is printed in *Boletín Acad. de Hist.* (1926).

Since the publication of this book, two important works have appeared which cast new light on the society of the later eighteenth century: Richard Herr, *The Eighteenth Century Revolution in Spain* (1958) and A. Domínguez Ortiz, *La sociedad española en el siglo XVIII* (1955); pp. 77–123 and 299–343 of the latter bear directly on the subject.

There is an admirable modern summary in J. Vicens Vives *Historia social y económica de España y América*, Vol. IV, Part i.

J. Sarrailh, *L'Espagne eclairée du XVIIIᵉ siècle* (1954) is an exhaustive treatment of *las luces* from the French point of view; P. Vilar's *La Catalogne dans l'Espagne moderne* (1962) is a masterly work of which Vol. II contains material on Catalan social structure.

For the earlier history of the aristocracy in New Castile see Noël Salomon, *La Campagne de Nouvelle Castille à la Fin du XVIᵉ Siècle* (1964).

4. LOMBARDY

For the study of the Lombard nobility two standard reference works are indispensable. These are the *Famiglie notabili milanesi* of F. Calvi (Milan, 1881), and Litta's *Famiglie celebri d' Italia* (Milan, 1819–81). Both are rich in genealogical and other information. Also useful is the *Dizionario Storico Blasonico delle famiglie nobili e notabili italiane* (Pisa, 1888). But there is no modern study of the subject. *Il patriziato milanese* by F. Calvi (Milan, n.d.) deals with the Patrician class, and is old-fashioned and unsystematic, but is still the best survey of any part of the nobility. Reference should also be made to this author's articles in the *Archivio Storico Lombardo* of 1874.

There are some useful books and articles on separate aspects of the subject. For the political background see F. Valsecchi's two volumes on *L' assolutismo illuminato in Austria e Lombardia* (Bologna, 1934), and the old but informative *Storia di Milano dall' origine a nostri giorni* of F. Cusani (Milan, 1867). On the same topic C. Morandi's *Idee e formazioni politiche in Lombardia, 1748-1814* (Pavia, 1927) is valuable, and is supplemented by his article on 'La fine del domino spagnuolo in Lombardia', *Archivio Storico Lombardo* (1936). The social and economic setting is best described in *Il settecento milanese* by C. A. Vianello (Milan, 1934), an author who has published several works on eighteenth-century Lombard history. His article on 'Il senato di Milano organo della dominazione straniera', *Archivio Storico Lombardo* (1936), should be consulted. E. Rota's *L' Austria in Lombardia* (Rome, 1911) is written from a strongly nationalist viewpoint, and is of less value than its reputation would suggest.

Several books illuminate the life of the *palazzi*. Two useful biographies are *Parini e la Lombardia nel secolo passato* by C. Cantù (Milan, 1852), and Valeri's *Pietro Verri* (Milan, 1937). But a more lively picture can be obtained from such contemporary material as the *Lettere e scritti inediti di Pietro ed Allessandro Verri*, ed. F. Casati (Milan, 1879), and the complete *Carteggio* of the same brothers, the publication of which began in 1910 and has now reached its ninth volume. Also entertaining are the *Memorie* of G. Gorani, ed. A. Casati (Milan, 1936, and still in process of publication).

5. PRUSSIA

General Works

The most useful single volume on the whole subject of the political and economic importance of the Prussian nobility at this period, especially in its relations with the Hohenzollern dynasty, is O. Hintze, *Die Hohenzollern und ihr Werk* (Berlin, 1915). Other general or biographical studies which are incidentally of value include: M. Braubach, 'Der Aufstieg Brandenburg-Preussens, 1640 bis 1815', in *Geschichte der führenden Völker*, vol. XV (Freiburg, 1933), pp. 165-367; F. Schnabel, 'Das 18. Jahrhundert in Europa' in *Propyläen-Weltgeschichte*, vol. VI (Berlin, 1931); L. Tümpel, *Entstehung des Brandenburgisch-Preussichen Einheitsstaats im Zeitalter des Absolutismus* (Berlin, 1915); R. Ergang, *The Potsdam Führer, Frederick William I* (New York, 1941); G. Ritter, *Friedrich der Grosse* (Leipzig, 1936); R. Koser, *Geschichte Friedrichs des Grossen* (the classical biographical study), 7th edn. (4 vols., Berlin, 1921-5); F.

Meinecke, *Das Zeitalter der deutschen Erhebung, 1795–1815* (Leipzig, 1946); *Weltbürgertum und Nationalstaat*, 6th edn. (Munich, 1922); G. Ritter, *Stein, eine politische Biographie* (2 vols., Stuttgart-Berlin, 1931); F. Schnabel, *Freiherr vom Stein* (Berlin and Leipzig, 1931); *Deutsche Geschichte im XIX. Jahrhundert*, vol. I (Freiburg, 1929).

Special Studies

E. Schwenke, *Friedrich der Grosse und der Adel* (Burg, 1911) was the first detailed treatment of Frederick's relations with the nobility. The outstanding monograph, on the social and economic side, is F. Martiny, *Die Adelsfrage in Preussen vor 1806 als politisches und soziales Problem* (Stuttgart-Berlin, 1938).

Political and Administrative

F. Hartung, 'Die Epochen der absoluten Monarchie in der neueren Geschichte', *Historische Zeitschrift*, vol. CXLV (1932), pp. 46–52; W. L. Dorn, 'The Prussian Bureaucracy in the XVIIIth Century', *Political Science Quarterly*, vol. XLVI (1931), pp. 403–23; vol. XLVII (1932), pp. 75–94 and 259–73; O. Hintze, 'Die Hohenzollern und der Adel', *Hist. Zeitschrift*, vol. CXII (1914), pp. 494–524; 'Preussische Reformbestrebungen vor 1806', *ibid.* vol. LXXVI (1896), pp. 413–43; G. Schmoller, *Das politische Testament Friedrich Wilhelms I von 1722* (Berlin, 1896); G. B. Volz, *Die politischen Testamente Friedrichs des Grossen* (Berlin, 1920).

Social and Economic

W. H. Bruford, *Germany in the Eighteenth Century: the Social Background to the Literary Revival* (Cambridge, 1935); H. Brunschwig, *La Crise de l'état Prussien à la fin du XVIIIe siècle et la genèse de la mentalité romantique* (Paris, 1947); J. H. Clapham, *Economic History of France and Germany*, 2nd edn. (Cambridge, 1923); F. L. Carsten, 'The Origins of the Junkers', *English Historical Review*, vol. LXII (1947), pp. 145–78; G. F. Knapp, *Die Bauernbefreiung und der Ursprung der Landarbeiter in den älteren Teilen Preussens*, pts. 1 and 2 (Leipzig, 1887); F. Grossmann, *Über die gutsherrlich-bäuerlichen Rechtsverhältnisse in der Mark Brandenburg vom 16. bis 18. Jahrhundert* (Leipzig, 1890); G. Aubin, *Zur Geschichte der gutsherrlich-bäuerlichen Verhältnisses in Ostpreussen von der Gründung des Ordenstaates bis zur Steinschen Reform* (Leipzig, 1911).

The following works dealing either directly or indirectly with the Prussian nobility in the eighteenth century have appeared since 1953: G. A. Craig, *The Politics of the Prussian Army, 1640–1945* (Oxford 1955); H. Rosenberg, *Bureaucracy, Aristocracy and Autocracy: the Prussian Experience, 1660–1815* (Harvard Historical Monographs. XXXIV, Cambridge Mass., 1958); F. L. Carsten, *Princes and Parliaments in Germany. From the fifteenth century to the eighteenth century* (Oxford, 1959); K. Demeter, *Das Deutscher Officierkorps im Gesellschaft und Staat, 1650–1945* (English translation: *The German Officer-Corps in Society and State*, London, 1965) and W. O. Henderson, *Studies in the Economic Policy of Frederick the Great* (London, 1963).

6. AUSTRIA

The Austrian equivalent of the English *Dictionary of National Biography* deserves pride of place: Constant von Wurzbach, *Biographisches Lexikon des Kaiserthums Österreich* (60 vols., Vienna, 1856–91). The most important primary source is the Lord High Steward's diary: Prince Johann Josef Khevenhüller-Metsch, *Tagebuch, 1742–1776* (7 vols. so far published, Vienna, 1907-25).

Notable general works containing incidental information on the subject in question are: Alfred von Arneth, *Maria Theresias erste Regierungsjahre* (3 vols., Vienna, 1863-5); the same author's *Geschichte Maria Theresias* (10 vols., Vienna, 1863-79); Adam Wolf, *Geschichtliche Bilder aus Österreich*, vol. II (Vienna, 1880); Paul Mitrofanov, *Joseph II. Seine politische und kulturelle Tätigkeit* (transl. from the Russian) (2 vols., Vienna-Leipzig, 1910); F. M. Mayer, H. Pirchegger, *Geschichte und Kulturleben Deutschösterreichs von 1526 bis 1792*, vol. II (Vienna-Leipzig, 1931).

As to reports of foreign travellers, cf. that by the Venetians Giovanni Andrea and Giovanni Benedetto Giovanelli, an extract of which appears in Dengel, 'Ein Kulturbild von Alt-Wien vor 200 Jahren', *Unsere Heimat*, vol. XVII (Vienna, March 1946); Mary Wortley Montagu, *Letters* (available in Everyman edition); Nathaniel W. Wraxall, *Memoirs of the Courts of Berlin, Dresden, Warsaw, and Vienna* (2 vols., Dublin, 1799); Henry Swinburne, *The Courts of Europe at the Close of the Last Century*, vol. I (London, 1895); M. L. Dutens, *Journal of Travels made through the Principal Cities of Europe* (transl. from the French) (London, 1782); E. Vehse, *Memoirs of the Court, Aristocracy, and Diplomacy of Austria* (transl. from the German, strong anti-Austrian bias) (2 vols., London, 1856); Johann Georg Forster, *Sämmtliche Schriften*, vol. VII (Leipzig, 1843).

For the administrative reforms, cf. F. Walter, 'Die ideellen

Grundlagen der österreichischen Staatsreform von 1749', *Zeitschrift für öffentliches Recht*, vol. XVII (1937); and by the same author, 'Der letzte grosse Versuch einer Verwaltungsreform unter Maria Theresia (1764-65)', *Mitteilungen des österreichischen Instituts für Geschichtsforschung*, vol. XLVII (1933).

For the Central European form of land-trust holdings, cf. O. Gierke, art. 'Fideikommisse' (Geschichte und Recht), in *Handwörterbuch der Staatswissenschaften*, vol. III (Jena, 1892); for the Austrian form in particular, S. Adler, *Zur Rechtsgeschichte des adeligen Grundbesitzes in Österreich* (Leipzig, 1902).

The history of a renowned noble family is traced in Jakob von Falke, *Geschichte des fürstlichen Hauses Liechtenstein* (2 vols., Vienna, 1868 and 1877); the life of a great soldier in Wilhelm von Janko, *Laudons Leben* (Vienna, 1869).

For Freemasons, cf. Ludwig Lewes, *Geschichte der Freimaurerei in Österreich und Ungarn* (Leipzig, 1872). The pseudo-conversions are the butt of an anonymous contemporary satire written between 1737 and 1739; cf. Max Braubach, 'Eine Satire auf den Wiener Hof aus den letzten Jahren des Kaisers Karls VI', *Mitteilungen des österreichischen Instituts für Geschichtsforschung*, vol. LIII (1939).

For the life of the reformer Sonnenfels, cf. Franz Kopetzky, *Josef und Franz von Sonnenfels* (Vienna, 1882).

For Bohemia, cf. T. V. Bílek, *Dějiny konfiskací v Čechách po roku 1618* (2 vols., Prague, 1882-3); Ernest Denis, *La Bohème depuis la Montagne-Blanche*, vol. I (Paris, 1903); R. J. Kerner, *Bohemia in the Eighteenth Century* (New York, 1930); Bartenstein's *Memoir über die innere Verfassung Böhmens, Mährens und Schlesiens, 1759* (Haus-, Hof- und Staatsarchiv, Vienna); Heinrich Benedikt, *Franz Anton Graf von Sporck. Zur Kultur der Barockzeit in Böhmen* (Vienna, 1923). For the link between the social history and the development of baroque architecture in the Bohemian capital, cf. Oskar Schürer, *Prag. Kultur, Kunst, Geschichte*, 2nd edn. (Vienna-Leipzig-Prague, 1935), containing well-chosen illustrations.

For aristocratic palaces in the Imperial capital, cf. Justus Schmidt, *Wien* (Vienna, 1947), equally well illustrated.

For the nobility's part in the musical life, cf. Karl von Dittersdorf, *Autobiography* (transl. from the German) (London, 1896); Dr Charles Burney, *The Present State of Music in Germany, the Netherlands, and United Provinces*, 2nd edn. (London, 1775); the relevant part on Austria is now available in German translation in a critical, annotated edition entitled *Musikalische Reise durch das alte Österreich* (1772) (Vienna, 1948).

For a general work on the social life of the nobility in Europe, cf. A. von Gleichen-Russwurm, *Das galante Europa. Geselligkeit der grossen Welt, 1600-1789* (Stuttgart, 1911); upper class life in Vienna is described in chapters VIII, XIX, XXIX. The recent book by Robert A. Kann, *A Study in Austrian Intellectual History from Late Baroque to Romanticism* (London, 1960) contains an important chapter on Joseph von Sonnenfels.

7. HUNGARY

The history, constitutional and general, of the Hungarian nobility is so intimately bound up with that of Hungary as a whole that no separate study of it has ever been made. The great codification of the noble's rights, Wérböczy's *Tripartitum*, completed in 1514 and reprinted many times since, set out the position in his day and was still regarded in the eighteenth century as representing it. The works of H. Marczali, *Ungarische Verfassungsgeschichte* (Tübingen, 1910) and *Ungarisches Verfassungrecht (ibid.*, 1911) are still the best works on their fields in any language outside Hungarian, and their conclusions have indeed been only slightly modified by later Hungarian writers. The same writer's *Hungary in the XVIIIth Century* (Cambridge, 1910), a translation of the introductory volume of his work on Joseph II, is, again, the best descriptive account in any language except Hungarian of the position in the eighteenth century. Vol. IV of the *Magyar Történet* by B. Hóman and G. Szekfü, 2nd edn. (Budapest, 1935), deals with the eighteenth century. Its bibliography refers to many source-works. B. Grünwald, *A Régi Magyarország* (Budapest, 1888), is an older work, especially devoted to and strongly critical of the nobility, to which L. Mocsáry replied in 1889 in *A Régi Magyar Nemes*, defending the class.

See also C. A. Macartney, *Hungary: A Short History* (Edinburgh, 1962).

8. SWEDEN

A general, modern bibliography of Swedish history is Samuel E. Bring, *Bibliografisk handbok till Sveriges historia* (Stockholm, 1934). Most valuable guides to the *état des questions* in the period 1718-92 are Hugo Valentin, *Frihetstiden inför eftervärlden* (Stockholm, 1942), and Georg Landberg, *Gustaf III i eftervärldens dom* (Stockholm, 1945).

The fundamental, pioneering work on the social structure of the nobility, without which this essay could not have been written, is Sten Carlsson's *Ståndssamhälle och ståndspersoner, 1700-1865* (Lund, 1949), which should be read in conjunction with the review in *Historisk Tidskrift*, 1950, by Walfrid Enblom, with the article in the same journal for 1951 by Per-Erik Brolin, entitled 'Ståndsutjämningen som historisk problem', and with Carlsson's note in *Historisk Tidskrift*, 1950. From these, all statistical information in the above essay is borrowed. A later, more popular book by Sten Carlsson, slightly modifying some of his earlier conclusions, is *Svensk ståndscirkulation, 1680-1950* (Uppsala, 1950). Sven Ulric Palme, *Stånd och klasser i forna dagars Sverige* (Stockholm, 1947), is popular and provocative, and should be used with caution.

For the political theory and constitutional ideas of the nobility, see above all Fredrik Lagerroth, *Frihetstidens författning. En studie i den svenska konstitutionalismens historia* (Stockholm, 1917) and *id. Konung och Adel. Ett bidrag till Sveriges författningshistoria under Gustav III* (Stockholm, 1917). For the Nobility as an Estate, and for parliamentary history, Hugo Valentin, *Frihetstidens Riddarhus. Några bidrag till dess karakteristik* (Stockholm, 1915); Fredrik Lagerroth, J. E. Nilsson, Ragnar Olsson, *Frihetstidens maktägande ständer, 1719-1772*, I-II (Stockholm, 1934) and, Georg Landberg, *Riksdagen under den gustavianska tiden* (Stockholm, 1932), together forming vols. V-VII of the collective work *Sveriges riksdag*; Lennart Linnarsson, *Riksrådens licentiering. En studie i frihetstidens parlamentarism* (Uppsala, 1943); [ed.] Carl Hallendorff, *Sveriges Riddarhus. Riddarskapet och adeln och dess Riddarhus* (Stockholm, 1926). On the nobility as an office-holding class, P. J. Edler, *Om börd och befordran under frihetstiden* (Stockholm, 1915); Ingvar Elmroth, *Nyrekryteringen till de högre ämbetena 1720-1809* (Lund, 1962). On the privileges of the nobility, W. Enblom, *Privilegiestriderna vid frihetstidens början. Ett bidrag till ståndsutjämningens historia* (Uppsala, 1925); E. Ingers, *Bonden i svensk historia*, II (Stockholm, 1948), for the obligations of their tenants. For their share in parochial self-government (on which it was not possible to touch within the compass of the above essay), K. H. Johansson, *Svensk sockensjälvstyrelse, 1686-1862* (Lund, 1937). For economic history in general and the economic strength of the nobility, Eli F. Heckscher, *Sveriges ekonomiska historia från Gustav Vasa*, II (Stockholm, 1949); Kurt Samuelsson, *De stora köpmanshusen i Stockholm, 1730-1815* (Stockholm, 1951), for capital investment in industry and trade; Birger Planting, *Baroner och patroner. Porträtt ur Sveriges jordbrukshistoria. 1700-talet* (Stockholm, 1944) for studies of noble agronomists. For cultural history in general, the collective work *Svenska folket genom tiderna*, vols. VI (*Frihetstidens kultur*) and VII (*Den gustavianska kulturen*) (Malmö, 1938); Ludvig Stavenow, *Frihetstiden. Dess epoker och kulturlif* (Göteborg, 1907); Sigrid Leijonhufvud, *Carl Gustaf Tessin och hans Åkerökrets*, I-II (Stockholm, 1931, 1933); E. N. Tigerstedt, *Svensk litteraturhistoria* (Stockholm, 1948) (with invaluable bibliography). For the detail about Åkerhielm, Birger Sallnäs, *Samuel Åkerhielm d.y.* (Lund, 1947). For Goodricke's expenditure, State Papers Foreign (Sweden) 95/104/ 254-5.

9. POLAND

S. Askenazy, *Józef Poniatowski* (Warsaw, 1905).

R. N. Bain, *The Last King of Poland* (London, 1909).

A. B. Boswell, *Poland and the Poles* (London, 1919).

Cambridge History of Poland (2 vols.) (Cambridge, 1941, 1950).

W. Coxe, *Travels into Poland*, etc. (3 vols., Dublin, 1874).

L. Dembicki, *Pulawy* (Lwów, 1887-88).

L. Engeström, *Minnen och anteckningar* (Stockholm, 1876).

W. Konopczyński, *Polska w dobie wojny siedmioletniej* (Warsaw, 1908-11).

T. Korzon, *Wewnentrzne dzieje Polski, 1764-94* (Cracow, 1897-8).

K. Koźmian, *Pamientniki, 1780-1815* (3 vols., Posen, 1858).

R. H. Lord, *The Second Partition of Poland* (Cambridge, U.S.A., 1915).

A. Mickiewicz, *Pan Tadeusz* (Lwów, 1909).

M. Ogiński, *Mémoires sur la Pologne, 1788-1815* (4 vols., Paris, 1826-7).

W. J. Rose, *Poland Old and New* (London, 1948).

W. Smolenski, *Przewrót umyslowy w Polsce wieku xviii* (Cracow, 1891).

S. Staszic, *Uwagi nad życiem Jana Zamoyskiego* (Cracow, 1861).

K. Waliszewski, *Potoccy i Czartoryscy, 1735-63* (Cracow, 1887).

N. W. Wraxall, *Memoirs of the Courts of Berlin, Warsaw*, etc., 1777-79 (2 vols., London, 1806).

Additional Bibliography
(By L. R. Lewitter, Fellow of Christ's College Cambridge)

J. Chałasiński, *Przeszłość i przyszłość inteligencji polskiej,* (Warsaw,

1958). *The past and the future of the Polish intelligentsia*. Includes chapters on the 'social genealogy' of the intelligentsia, that is on its descent from the *szlachta*.

A. Ciechanowiecki, *Michał Kazimierz Ogiński und sein Musenhof zu Słonim. Untersuchungen zur Geschichte der polnischen Kultur und ihrer europäischen Beziehungen im 18. Jahrhundert* (Cologne, 1961).

W. Czapliński, 'Rządy oligarchii w Polsce nowożytnej', *Przegląd Historyczny*, vol. LII, no. 3 (1961), pp. 445–63. Summary in French pp. 464–65. 'The rule of the oligarchy in Poland between the sixteenth and the eighteenth century.'

S. Czarnowski, 'La réaction catholique en Pologne à la fin du XVIe et au début du *XVIIe* siècle', *La Pologne au VIIe Congrès International des Sciences Historiques*, vol. II (Warsaw, 1933), pp. 287–310.

W. Dworzaczek, *Genealogia*, 2 vols. (Warsaw, 1959). Tables and detailed introduction with numerous bibliographical references. A fundamental work.

W. Dworzaczek, 'Kto w Polsce dzierżył buławy?', *Przegląd Historyczny*, vol. XXXIX (1949), pp. 163–70. No summary 'On the holders of the office of commander-in-chief between the sixteenth and the eighteenth centuries.'

W. Dworzaczek, 'Przenikanie szlachty do mieszczaństwa w XVI i XVII w.', *ibid.*, vol. XLVII (1956), pp. 656–84. Summary in French pp. 831–32.' The penetration of the *szlachta* into the bourgeoisie in the sixteenth and seventeenth centuries.'

O. Hoetzsch, 'Adel und Lehnwesung in Russland und Polen und ihr Verhältnis zur deutscher Entwicklung', *Historische Zeitschrift*, vol. CVIII (1912), pp. 571–87.

S. Konarski, *Armorial de la noblesse polonaise titrée* (Paris, 1958). A scholarly work.

G. Rhode, 'Staaten-Union und Adelsstaat', *Zeitschrift für Ostforschung*, IX (1960), pp. 185–215.

P. Skwarczyński, 'The problem of feudalism in Poland up to the beginning of the sixteenth century', *The Slavonic and East European Review*, vol. XXXIV (1958), pp. 292–310.

A. Wyczański, *Studia nad folwarkiem szlacheckim w Polsce w latach 1500–1580* (Warsaw, 1960). Summarized as 'L'économie du domaine nobiliaire moyen 1500–1580' in *Annales. Economies-Sociétés-Civilisations*, vol. XVIII¹ (1963), pp. 81–7.

A. Zajączkowski. *Główne elementy kultury szlacheckiej w Polsce . . .*,

Wrocław, 1961 [reproduced from typescript], summarized as 'Cadres structurales de la noblesse', *ibid.*, pp. 88–102.

10. RUSSIA

The history of the Russian nobility is so inseparable from that of Russian society as a whole that it must primarily be studied in its general setting. See B. H. Summer, *Survey of Russian History* (London, 2d ed. 1947). For bibliographical surveys see also A. G. Mazour, *Modern Russian Historiography* (2nd ed. 1958); C. Morley, *Guide to Research in Russian History* (1951).

Important works in English are: W. F. Reddaway (ed.), *Documents of Catherine the Great* (1931); M. Raeff, *Michael Speransky* (1957); R. Pipes (ed.), *Karamzin's Memoir on Ancient and Modern Russia* (1959); H. Rogger, *National Consciousness in Eighteenth Century Russia* (1960); J. Blum, *Lord and Peasant in Russia* (1961).

There are some important writings in French on the economic aspects of the subject: A. Miller, *Essai sur l'histoire des institutions agraries de la Russie centrale du XVIᵉ au XVIIIᵉ siècles* (1926); R. Portal, 'Manufactures et classes sociales en Russie au XVIIIᵉ siècle', *Revue Historique* (1949); *L'Oural au XVIIIᵉ siècle* (1950); M. Confins, *Domaines et seigneurs en Russia vers la fin du XVIIIᵉ siècle* (1963).

Russian works besides the standard history of V. O. Klyuchevsky include: A. V. Romanovich-Slavatinskii, *Dvoriantstvo v Rossii ot Nachala XVIII veka* (*The Russian Nobility from the Beginning of the Eighteenth Century* (2nd ed. 1912); S. A. Korf, *Dvoriantstvo i ego sosolvnoe upravlenie za stolete 1762–1855 godov* (*The Nobility and its Corporate Organization in the Century 1762–1855*) (1906); D. A. Korsakov, *Votsarenie Imperatritsy Anny Ioannovny* (*The Accession of the Empress Anne*) (1880); *Iz zhizni russkikh deatelei XVIII veka* (*From the Lives of Russian Workers in the Eighteenth Century*) (1891); N. Chechulin, *Russkoe Provintsialnoe Obstchestvo vo Vtoroi Polovine XVIII veka* (*Russian Provincial Society in the Second Half of the Eighteenth Century*) (1889).

For the composition of the nobility and an account of the principal families see P. Dolgorukov, *Rossiiskaya rodoslovnaya kniga* (*Russian Genealogical Book*) (4 vols. 1854–1857); A. Kleinschmidt, *Russlands Geschichte und politik dargestellt in der russischen hohen Adels* (Cassel. 1877). Soviet historiography has not contributed a great deal, but see P. I. Lyaschenko, *History of the National Economy of Russia to the 1917 Revolution* (Engl. transl. New York, 1949) and the relevant volumes of *Ocherki istorii SSSR* (*Outlines of the History of the USSR*).

The suggested revision of the older version of Catherine's policy can be found in a series of articles by the German historian G. Sacke: 'Adel und Bürgertum in der Regierungszeit Katharinas II von Russland', *Revue Belge de Philologie et d'Histoire*, XVII (1938); 'Zur Charakteristik der gesetzgebenden Kommission Katharinas II von Russland', *Archiv für Kulturgeschichte*, XXI (1931); 'Katharina II im Kampf um Thron und Selbstherrschaft', *ibid.*, XXIII (1932); 'Adel und Bürgertum in der gesetzgebenden Kommission Katharinas II von Russland', *Jahrbücher für Geschichte Osteuropas*, III (1938).